FOUR BOYS, TWO CANOES, and THE GUADALUPE RIVER

From Comfort to the Coast of Texas with
Don Durden, James Durden, Peter Krauter, and Mark Rausch

Mae Durden-Nelson

EAKIN PRESS Fort Worth, Texas

This book is dedicated to all teenage boys
who not only dream dreams of adventure,
but are lucky enough to follow them
and live to tell the story!

The maps shown in this book are copies of the actual Texas Department of Transportation (TxDOT) 1971 county maps and are being used with copyright permission. There were five sets of these maps, one set for each canoe and one set for parents.

Copyright © 2007
By Mae Darden-Nelson
Published By Eakin Press
An Imprint of Wild Horse Media Group
P.O. Box 331779
Fort Worth, Texas 76163
1-817-344-7036
www.EakinPress.com
ALL RIGHTS RESERVED
1 2 3 4 5 6 7 8 9
ISBN-10: 1-934645-22-2
ISBN-13: 978-1-934546-22-2
Library of Congress Control Number 2007000000

Contents

Introduction

The most surprising factor about this book is that it took thirty-five years before someone would think to make public the intrinsic worth of this story. The idea to write the story came from Diana Drenner, the sister of Mark Rausch. Once she planted the seed and the story recalled, the writing became imperative, especially since her brother, Mark, recently died of cancer and, of the three sets of parents, only one father and one mother are still living.

I thank Diana (Rausch) Drenner for giving the needed nudge to birth the idea of this book. I immediately contacted the three remaining players in this adventure to ask if the idea of a book might also intrigue them. Receiving a unanimous yes, my husband and I invited them to dine with us in our home. I set a tape recorder in the middle of the table. We sat down to eat at six-thirty and did not move again until almost midnight. The stories flowed like fine wine as Peter played his laptop presentation of the eighty pictures he had taken thirty-five years ago during their canoe trip down the Guadalupe. The room rocked with laughter at remembered antics as they recalled their daring deeds that in retrospect brought abrupt silence and a head shaking, "We could have been killed!"

At one point, late in the evening, my sons turned to me to ask, "Mom! What were you thinking?" It was impossible to answer and so they answered themselves. "It was a different time then. We were so lucky to grow up in a time and an atmosphere that could permit such an idea as a canoe trip down the Guadalupe River by teenagers!" Their answer then prompted another period of sad reflective silence. *Are those days really gone forever?* We agreed we had a book that needed publication.

I accepted the challenge to write it since I am the only mother left and am an author too. I confess I found it difficult to write this story without adding my personal interjections and comments. For, while those four boys had their adventures, *we parents had our account too!* I remember how thirty-five years ago, once we had given our consent to this adventure, that even while we then became the *praying* cheerleaders of their odyssey, we were frightened for them beyond the telling!

It is important then to make clear how this story comes down

Don Durden, second from left, describes an intense moment as he recalls an episode from their 1971 canoe trip. Around the table in rapt attention are, left to right, Mae Durden-Nelson, Don Durden, Susan Durden, Monica Wallace, James Durden, and Peter Krauter.

to you after all these years. First, you will *see* and *experience* their adventures through their own individual *on-the-scene* observances from Don and Peter as each kept awesome and most proficient daily journals. Their innocent writings—written when they were seventeen and fifteen—make the details of the upcoming daily episodes riveting. I salute their Comfort High School English teachers for the obvious well-taught vocabulary usage and the command of the language they display. It is now ours to enjoy. I have edited almost nothing from their writings with the exception of inserting only a few punctuation marks. Today, Peter, now doing research at Texas A&M says this, "My canoe mate, Mark Rausch, paddled solo around the next bend much too early in life but thankfully through this writing, Mark is very much alive in our story."

Finally, placing the cream on top of the cake, James Durden—only 15 at the time—supplies us with remarkable recall narratives. He too paints colorful and superb *first person* accounts for our reading pleasure and edification. He too is a writer of merit!

I want to express thanks to Don Durden, James Durden, and Peter Krauter for permitting me the honor to compile their stories into this book.

At the end of their story, you may also be interested in the biographies of all four. Information on the Mark Rausch bio came from his sister, Diana Drenner and also from Jim Moore, Comfort barber. Visiting with him one afternoon, Jim spoke from a long time adult friendship with Mark. Jim reiterated the wonderful humor and down-home personality that remained with Mark into his adult years. Thank you for that, Jim! The circle was then complete.

Following their biographies, each remaining canoe trip participant also submitted to me their perspective for inclusion at the end of this book. Because the journey *was what it was*, it seemed important to publish how they—now successful and mature businessmen and currently parents themselves—how they view their canoe trip experience from today's mature dis-

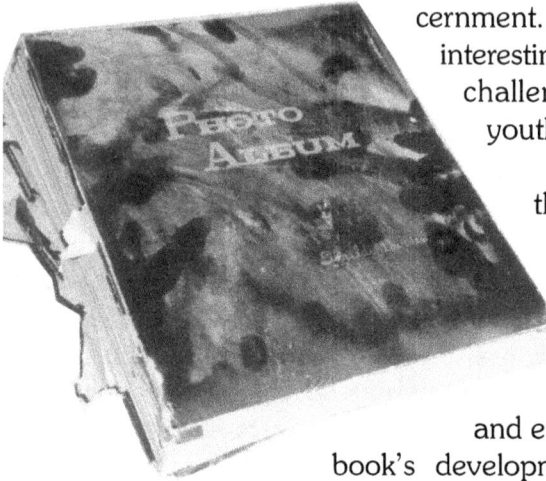

cernment. You will find them interesting, encouraging, and challenging for today's youth.

Finally, I want to thank and acknowledge my incredible and awesome husband, Bill Nelson, for his consistent support and encouragement in this book's development. To add even more detail to his story, Bill struggled patiently for several days over the original, well-used, and badly soiled 1971 county maps so that they could be included in this book and would correspond from day one to the end of the journey showing each day's paddled progress down the Guadalupe. Through Bill's work, an authentic map will appear at the end of each appropriate chapter and show where the boys spent that night. These maps will also help the reader to scrutinize the Guadalupe River as it so uniquely twists and turns its way to the coast for some 500 miles.

Then there are Peter's original pictures! The photographic technology of 1971 is admittedly not today's fine art. Nevertheless, linger over them a while, put yourself into the scene, and allow your imagination to soar.

I invite you now to savor the chronicles of four teenage boys, two canoes and the Guadalupe River—take the journey back into a world that sadly no longer exists.

—MAE DURDEN-NELSON
Comfort, Texas

1

The Early Years

Forty-seven years ago on the outskirts of the small Texas hill country village of Comfort there were *seventeen* boys of varying ages living in a three-block area in a nice, middle class neighborhood known as Oakcrest. There were also nine girls but they didn't mix much with the boys back then.

For many summers to come, those seventeen boys wandered the neighborhood from one yard to another, always dreaming up *stuff* to do. They built forts and enacted play battles with dirt clumps and other harmless objects. There were lengthy games of hide and seek and one memorable day one of the Durden boys hid in a small chicken coop in the Thomas's backyard—not aware that a yellow jacket nest was over the door. The enormous yowl broke up their fun and the kids all watched while Ruth Thomas applied whatever to make the stings go away. Ruth was good at that sort of thing because seven kids were hers and somebody was always getting cuts and scratches.

Don and James Durden lived in the middle of that three-block area. Their unfenced backyard contained a huge 20' x 20' sandbox that had nice working swings and stuff. But, Tonka toys were favored and imaginations knew no bounds. For hours on end, the sand became a city under construction and they built roads and tunnels and bridges and then they'd get the water hose and make rivers to run through the entire make-believe town. Finally, someone would whisper the idea to *blow it all up—bombard it all with large rocks!* Then, amid uproarious laughter, mud and sand would fly helter skelter! Later when the boys went home and left sand and mud tracks in their individual homes, there were reprimands from the moms of the neighborhood. Meanwhile, Don and James had to clean all the rocks out of the sand. But it was worth it!

There were also competitions using Peter Krauter's huge vacant lot as a baseball field. Word was sent around the neighborhood and in no time a game was underway. No adult ever supervised the activity.

Interestingly, every one of these boys had television in their homes but it was seldom watched—especially during the day. Being outdoors provided much more fun.

The boys also played in the streets since Oakcrest was on the outskirts of town and the only people driving there were the fathers going to work and two or three of the kids old enough to drive.

The boys also knew that they could wander into any one of their houses and know they'd be welcomed with cookies and Kool Aid. Their mothers were all friends—they were *at home*—and there was always one set of mom's eyes watching over them at any given time.

Eventually, several of them grew old enough to be in the school band. Fall evenings, out in any yard, one could hear different instrument sounds coming from all the various houses. The parents grimaced but smiled. Band was a proud tradition in Comfort's schools.

As the boys grew older, they enjoyed the freedom to ride their bicycles all over town where everyone knew them by name. Eventually, they all seemed to migrate to the nearby Guadalupe River to fish or swim or "just mess around." Life in this small town was good. The camaraderie and trust that developed between these youngsters and their parents was strong. It was a unique way to grow a boy.

By 1971, Peter Krauter, one of those in the neighborhood, was fifteen years old, the second youngest in his family of one brother and two sisters. Peter was from a prominent line of Texas pioneer families. Indeed, his was the leading family who had established not only the first bank in Comfort but was also among the largest landholders. They owned Ingenhuett's, the oldest mercantile store in Texas. Peter was a handsome, intellectual, quiet, responsible, young man. With an air much older than his years, he smiled somewhat at most childish things. But he was in no way a stand-off from the group. The boys all liked him and in their young eyes, they saw nothing different about Peter.

One block north, on South Street, lived the two Durden boys. Don was now seventeen, and James, like Peter, was fifteen. The three were classmates and friends at Comfort High and in the school band. Don was elected band president that year.

There was only eighteen months difference in age between Don and James and they were almost the same size. The big difference between them was personality. Don was the serious, confident, dark straight-haired leader-type. James was the comic, dark blonde curly-headed, *don't-sweat-the-small-stuff* youngster. Even though they shared a room, thankfully sleeping in separate twin beds, they were absolutely the odd couple. Don was the neat one; James was *what's-the-big-deal* type. However, don't anyone dare to harm or in any way threaten the other brother! Those two boys shared secrets, told lies to support each other, and generally stood shoulder to shoulder.

Since Don was the oldest, he may have been the ringleader or originator of their daring idea that summer of 1971.

Peter says no, it was always a dream that he'd had. He remembers —even as a small boy—he'd fish the Guadalupe River that runs by Comfort and when a small leaf would flow by— he'd daydream: *Lucky leaf! What all will that leaf see and hear as it flows on down the river?*

James Durden kind of rolls his eyes, shrugs his shoulders, and says he has no idea who thought of it first. "It wasn't me! I was just there and got involved by osmosis."

But to complete their vision concerning this river deal, they needed a fourth person. Tommy Burow, who lived out in the rural area, was supposed to have been the one, but he had some kind of unnamed health issue. Don says, "I guess we were smart enough to know that if he developed a problem along the way, we wouldn't know what to do." Therefore, they cast their eyes on skinny Mark Rausch, barely 17. He was new to the neighborhood, but he was a drummer in their school band and he was "that wild and crazy guy" they all liked. They agreed to offer Mark the fourth bean. He immediately took hold of the idea and thought it sounded *great!* Count him in! The four boys had their basic team.

There remained three obstacles: *Parents.* The Durdens' father was a telephone field engineer who traveled most every week. Mom would be the one to convince.

Peter's parents, known as Comfort's Ingenhuett's General Store people, were most likely to agree. Since his mom was locally famous for having earned her pilot's license as a young girl, Peter figured she would immediately see the adventure. He was not so sure about his more conservative dad. He'd ask him first.

Mark Rausch's parents were newcomers to the neighborhood but they seemed open-minded. His mother had a flower shop in Comfort and everybody in town knew his father—a skinny but wiry tough cowboy type who was in the business of buying, selling, and trading livestock. It was a toss-up how Mark's parents would react.

Whatever the outcome, the time had come to approach parents: *"We would like to take a canoe trip down the Guadalupe River—all the way to the Gulf of Mexico."*

Parental Discussions

"You want to do what!?"

That was pretty much the instant reaction from all the parents and discussions immediately followed between the mommas and the papas. Each confessed serious misgivings, listed many probable problems, and raised countless unanswered questions. There was the safety issue of such a venture. Were their sons mature enough to undertake such an ambitious idea? Did they even realize *how ambitious* an idea it is? Could they handle emergencies? All the unanswered questions finally prompted a call to Bob Roberts, a well-known outdoorsman living in Comfort and close friend of the Durden family.

"I can't believe it! You mean to tell me there are still boys that dream of stuff like that? I guess boys have not changed all that much."

"So, what do you think, Bob? Are boys this age able to make a canoe trip down the Guadalupe River *all the way to the coast*? They seem pretty determined."

"It will take more than determination. But, they don't know that and that's good. However, they do need some important education about practical things."

"You know what it takes to do this. Would you work with them for a few weeks?"

"I'll be happy to do that. I'll let you know what I think."

"We'll hold off giving them our answer until then. We appreciate your willingness to work with our boys, Bob. We're all pretty nervous about them just taking off on their own like that."

"I'm impressed that you parents didn't just say no immediately. There are some real dangers—you have to understand that."

"That's why we're asking for your help. We think our boys are rugged individuals and have a good level of intelligence between them. So don't hold back anything when you work with them. Bob, we are depending on your assessment of their abilities. Based on your final judgment is how we will decide."

"That's a lot of responsibility to heap on me, lady. And, I appreciate your confidence. But, you must also know this: Because I *am* acquainted with the great adventure that is ahead for those boys—should they take this trip—my decision *may be influenced by that*. I may *encourage* their venture in spite of the dangers and hazards they may face."

"I trust your sound judgment, Bob. We parents will stick together on this, be it *yes* or *no*."

"That's another consideration. If you say no, you surely know that someday they just might take off without your permission and then ..."

"How long will you need to work with them before you decide?"

"Three weeks—yes—three weeks should give me enough insight. At the end of that time, if they have listened and learned, I'll give you my decision."

Training and Tests

All the exact details of the next three weeks are sketchy at best and have become forever mixed into the adventure itself. There are recalled vague bits and pieces of lectures from Bob Roberts as remembered by the would-be adventurers.

"The Guadalupe's timeless passage across the limestone outcrops that characterize the topographic transition from the Edwards Plateau to the Coastal Plain has cut canyons through and around the hills. As a result, there are *unique deep erosions into those banks* and I need to warn you boys about the *whirlpools* that are prevalent where this has happened in the Guadalupe River. Careless canoers—caught in those strong pools—have been sucked under by them and drown. The good news for you is that the river is really down this year and that will make your journey safer than usual. The bad news concerning the *down* flow of the river is that you will need to portage your canoes a lot. That's not much fun—its hard work—you need to know that right off."

"Now if you go, you are all too young to carry pistols. But you need something for protection. I suggest each member of the party should arm himself with a four foot machete."

Mr. Roberts concluded one of his lectures by advising the

foursome to carry a well supplied first-aid kit. "Most important, two good snakebite kits and you *will also need to take* a needle and strong thread."

"What! Why?"

"When you read your river maps, you will see that for the last twenty or so miles before you reach the coast, there are almost no people living along that stretch of the river. Help will not be available if one of you gets cut. Someone will have to sew him up! It would be up to you to save his life. You think you could do that?"

The boys laugh as they look at each other—eyebrows raised—heads shaking back and forth. After a few moments of silence, James speaks with a definite hesitation in his voice. "Well—okay. But, I'm not sure I could do that—sew somebody up."

Bob's face is serious, "I'm *not kidding around*, guys. I'm telling you it is a possible situation. Think about it. If someone's life is at stake—hopefully one of you will do what you have to do."

Reluctantly, all four boys nodded and agreed. Internally they vowed to be especially careful those last miles of the trip. (*Little did they know ...*)

"Another important consideration when planning a river trip is to take along a good supply of Halizone tablets to treat and disinfect your drinking water. Halizone tablets will not kill tapeworm eggs although they may be effective against bacteria if used properly. Play it safe with your drinking water! The Guadalupe normally has good springs all along. But, like I've told you, the water level is low this year and that could mean that some of the springs are not running. *The Halizone tablets are a must. Don't ever drink the river water without the treatment no matter how thirsty you may be!* You do not want to get sick on this trip. So remember, when you find a good spring, drink your fill, and then refill your jugs before continuing down the river. Don't forget the Halizone."

"Another major factor will be river maps. I thought I might

be able to find some detailed Guadalupe River maps for you but none are available. So, you'll have to settle for detailed county maps. Don and James, those should be available through your dad's company. (Southwestern Engineering Company) It is important for you to keep your maps dry and you should study them daily—sometimes hourly. Nothing is worse than *not know-ing* where you are.

"Another aspect of the trip is whether to buy or borrow two canoes. After several trips to investigate the purchase of canoes—I would suggest you visit the Comfort Boy Scout Troop #101. I've talked to the scoutmaster in your behalf and he has agreed to loan you their two canoes. He will draw up a responsibility contract and you four boys and your parents will have to sign also.

"You should each buy your own paddles according to your size. Hold your hand flat in front of you with the palm down and place your index finger right at the tip of your nose. The correct length paddle would just fit into the palm of your hand with the blade standing on the ground directly in front of you. It's a guide I've used when selecting paddles from the store and it works. Also, you should each take one spare paddle."

Mr. Roberts' final assignment was to actually make several short canoe runs from Comfort to the Waring crossing ... about nine miles in distance. "From this exercise, you will know how much distance you could travel in x number of minutes. You will also experience the teamwork needed to paddle a canoe. Should you make this journey, you and your canoe mate will be spending a lot of time together. It's important you get along and work well together."

(It should be noted here that only Peter Krauter had attended Hermann Sons Youth Camp and had for several years taken canoeing where they were taught how to handle a canoe, and at the end of the week's session had competed in canoe skills.)

A James Durden Recollection ...
One of the greatest challenges for me occurred during one of

those practice runs. As the four of us neared our destination for that day (the bridge in Waring) we (the two canoes) got into a sprint paddling contest to see who would finish first. Not being as competitively compelled as the others, I let up with the heavy duty paddling right at the end and the other canoe ended up finishing first. Don was outraged. He told me if I didn't have the wherewithal to finish this little practice trip maybe I didn't have what it would take to make the real trip and that he would have to think about finding another partner. I was devastated. I *wanted to go* on this journey really bad and failed to see the correlation between this occurrence and the real trip.

Don and I spent a few days at odds with one another over this incident and only after promising honestly and earnestly to never "give up" during the trip was I allowed to rejoin the team. This occasion may have only been a test for Don to ensure I would be able to make the trip but it became a personal challenge to me as a motivational tool always to remind me what could be at stake if I ever faltered or decided to give in. I vowed inwardly to take every stroke of the paddle necessary to make it down the river and never once complain. I promised myself I would never give up or slack off and always try to be a benefit to the trip and not a hindrance.

The Decision

Three weeks to the day, the phone rang in the Durden home. Bob Roberts sounded serious. "If your schedule permits, I'd like to meet with you and our boys this afternoon out here at my house. Will that work for you?"

At two o'clock, assembled around Robert's bar on bar stools were Dr. Lamone Livingston, Bob Roberts, the Durden parents and sons, Don and James; also Peter Krauter and Mark Rausch. There was no small talk. The canoe trip decision was at hand.

"If you boys think that you still want to go on this journey— it is my opinion that you can handle a canoe trip to the coast. What I've seen of you boys gives me no reason to change my mind. I think you have the strength. I judge that you have the intelligence. You will need a lot of both. So, if your parents agree, I say set your date and get on with it. Make me proud of you. Once you've set your date to launch, please let me know? I want to be there to see you off. In the meantime, if you think of any more questions—or you need any help—just let me know. I'll help you all I can."

A Frenzy of Activity

Almost immediately, the boys visited Mr. Westmoreland, the local scoutmaster, to see about the loan of the Boy Scout's canoes. Fortunately, he was also a teacher at Comfort ISD and knew all four boys well enough to entrust them with the scout's canoes.

Comfort, Texas

May 27, 1971

To: BOY SCOUT TROOP # 101   Re: Two (2) canoes
    Comfort, Texas

By agreement of this paper, duly undersigned and notarized, the Boy Scout
Troop #101 of Comfort, Texas agrees to loan to the following persons two
(2) canoes which are the property of said Scout Troop #101. The terms of this
agreement shall be in effect from May 27, 1971 until said two (2) canoes are
returned to the scout troop # 101.

Donald Durden ,   _James Durden_
Donald Durden   James Durden
Peter Kreuter ,   _Mark Rausch_
Peter Kreuter   Mark Rausch

ALSO, We the undersigned Parents of the above named, do hereby promise to
underwrite and be responsible for any and all damages which might incur to
two (2) said canoes while on loan to above parties.

Mrs Jerry Durden Jr ,   _Mrs Jerry Durden, Jr_
Jerry Durden, Jr (for Donald Durden) Jerry Durden, Jr (for James Durden)
Mrs. James Kreuter ,   _Mrs Hubert Rausch_
James Kreuter (for Peter Kreuter)   Hubert Rausch, (for Mark Rausch)

ALSO, this agreement, undersigned and notarized, is accepted by me this day of
May 27, 1971; _Harrison Westmoreland_
              Harrison Westmoreland, Boy Scoutmaster Troop # 101

The State of Texas:
County of Kendall:

Before me, the undersigned authority in and for Kendall County, Texas, on this
day personally appeared Mrs. Jerry Durden, Mrs. James Kreuter, Mrs. Hubert
Rausch, and Harrison Westmoreland, known to me to be the person whose names
are subscribed to the foregoing instrument, and acknowledged to me that they
executed the same for the purposes and consideration therein expressed.

Given under my hand and seal of office this 27th day of May, 1971.

                              W. C. Kunkler
                     Notary Public, Kendall County, Texas

Getting It Together

Lessons in how to pack a canoe also came from Bob Roberts.

Peter Krauter remembers these details. "I only took two changes of clothes. I had two pairs of cut-off jeans, two sleeveless chambray shirts, and one pair of slip-on deck shoes. What I wasn't currently wearing was sealed with a twist-tie in one garbage bag, which was then sealed in a second garbage bag with a twist-tie, and placed in a large metal lard can. The lard can was tied to a cross-strut of the canoe so it wouldn't float off if we happened to turn over. Also, packed with my clothes inside the garbage bag were my two army blankets (one to lie on and one to lie under) and assorted food supplies which we didn't want to get wet. We also had metal army surplus ammo cans with waterproof lids where we kept other smaller items like my camera, our billfolds, and my notepad."

Peter continues, "Our other supplies—*I still have the receipt from the Army/Navy surplus store in San Antonio*—was my four-foot machete, one ammo can, and two army blankets. It all cost me a little over nine dollars! My camera was a Kodak Instamatic 44, which used 126 film, and cost $9.95.

"I splurged on my paddle, opting to buy only one. It was

Peter's 1971 receipt from the Army-Navy store in San Antonio

made of a solid piece of wood rather than strips of wood glued together. I think it cost around $15 from a shop in Kerrville.

Solid wood paddle with waterproof container for small items.

"Food provisions consisted of bread, many cans of tuna fish, Lipton's Onion Soup mix (the powdered kind you mix with water), canned beans, peaches, government surplus powdered eggs, peanut butter, and instant coffee. (*My brother Greg was working his way through Texas University at the time and he got these for us.*) We did have salt and pepper for seasoning. We only packed food that could be eaten cold or heated in a pot—no frying and each of us had aluminum mess kits with utensils included, and a set of nesting aluminum pots. We also had tin coffee cups for drinking water and coffee.

"If we had anything resembling a medical kit, it must have been in Don and James' canoe because I didn't even pack so much as a Band-Aid. Having grown-up in the outdoors and on the river, I wasn't worried much about snakes."

"Jerry Durden, Don and James's dad and Southwestern Engineering Company supplied the maps of all the Texas Counties that concerned the Guadalupe River. They were so detailed they even showed locations of water wells. Mr. Durden provided us with five sets of maps. A set for each canoe, and one set for each of our parents so they could track our progress down the river. The maps will also help us agree on rendezvous locations for our planned Sunday meetings with our parents when they will bring us new supplies and or whatever is needed."

"After a discussion with our parents, we set the launch date of our journey to begin Monday, June 7, 1971, at 8:00 A.M."

The Waring Crossing Launch
Monday, 8:00 A.M, June 7, 1971

Monday morning dawned cloudless and typically warm for early summer. At the beautiful Waring crossing, only a few miles out of Comfort, Hubert and Vera Rausch and their son Mark arrive with two canoes on board their pickup truck. Mae and Jerry Durden and their sons, Donald, James and eight-year-old little brother Roger get there about the same time. Gladys and James Krauter and son, Peter, pull in next. And even though it is early, Peter's grandfather, August Krauter, drives up to watch his grandson embark on this adventure. Peter remembers this most vividly: "This is the only memory I have of him being outside his house other than at Oma Krauter's funeral. He was a quiet man who never spoke much to me—even when I sat alone with him in his parlor waiting for my dad to pick me up after setting pins at the bowling alley just down the street. I was pretty impressed that Opa Krauter came."

If there are lingering misgivings on the parents' part, those thoughts are not spoken aloud. If the four boys, Don, James, Peter, and Mark have any last minute jitters, they are not evident.

The parents watch as their sons quickly unload the canoes

The Waring Crossing and preparing to launch

The canoes are loaded and are ready to launch

and place them near the water's edge. Supplies and all the para-phernalia needed for the next few weeks are loaded into the ca-noes. Lastly, the paddles are placed inside them and now all is ready.

Nervous laughter emanates from the three suddenly speech-less mothers standing in observance. An awkward silence hangs in the air. Finally, Mae Durden steps forward, "Don, I have a let-ter from Bob Roberts. He wants you to read it out loud before you launch."

"I'm disappointed. I really wanted him to be here," Don says regretfully as he steps up to accept the letter. Don reads:

June 6, 1971

Gentlemen:

It's 1 a.m. and I'm still working, so I can see I won't be there to see you off. Nevertheless, I can't stop thinking about you.

I wish 50,000 American young men could follow you, for they'd be better for it. No matter how this country, or any country, goes—to the right, to the left, to the hippies or the hard hats—there will be leaders. There will always be lead-ers. There will always be leaders and a leader is one who goes one step beyond his logical limitations and convinces others they can do the same. Perhaps when God said we were made in His image, He was only trying to tell us that we have almost the same equipment.

Am I making too much of this trip? I don't think so. You won't be threatened by wild beasts or Indians, but you will become tired and get dirty wet. A malted milk will be worth five dollars and the mosquitoes won't know you from your ancestors. You aren't your ancestors, either, and there's the rub—you are trying to create a few of their hardships, plac-ing yourselves just in a small way on their anvil to see if you can stand the stroke of the hammer. Good. Find out. This year, the Guadalupe; next year, more and tougher scholastic courses than you thought you could cut. Seven years from now give us a young politician who campaigns into the night scything down the odds.

Politically you may see the best road for this country as left, right, or down-the-middle. Not my concern. When you grab power, I'll be gone—dead or ineffective. Just don't let us be governed, ruled, by gabble and shriek, by the whims of the uninformed.

The odds are harder for you. It isn't enough to know the direction from Indianola to Fredericksburg and how to treaty with the Comanches. Yet someone has to lead. We can't go stumbling and snarling down three different roads, like confused animals. This is a nation.

The bad food, the strung sore muscles, wet clothes, insect bites, will be those small secret medals you pin inside yourselves, medals of significance only to you. But, not valueless. Someday you'll take them out and say, "If I did that …" Then you'll cram for another hour or scorn the muckrakers, and my country will have men leading it.

(signed) Bob

Almost in unison, the gathering reacts. "What an awesome letter!"

An awkward silence again settles over the group. Finally, Jerry Durden speaks, "Okay boys, I've got to get back to my office. But first, we've brought a bottle of champagne. We want to see you off with a toast."

The champagne emerges almost instantly. The cork pops. Plastic glasses are passed around and filled. Jerry Durden raises his glass, "Here's wishing you, Don, James, Peter, and Mark a safe and exciting journey. Bon Voyage!"

Everyone raises their glasses, "To a safe and exciting jour-

Don Durden reads the letter from Bob Roberts with the boys and Vera Rausch, Mark's mother listening.

ney." Even Grandpa Krauter seems to be getting into the spirit of the moment as he raises his glass and offers his own champagne toast! "I'm very proud of you boys. Be safe, Peter!"

Quickly, all gulp down the sparkling bubbly. There are good-byes all around and without hesitation the boys push off their two canoes at the Waring crossing, jump in and begin to paddle away—Don and James in one and Peter and Mark in the other. The parents watch in absolute quiet as in a matter of only minutes, the two canoes with their four young sons on board, vanish around a bend in the river and they are out of sight.

Someone in the crowd whispers softly, "Okay, folks. This is where we all better start praying."

Little brother Roger Durden tugs his father's hand, "Daddy, I wanted to go with them."

"So did I, son. So did I."

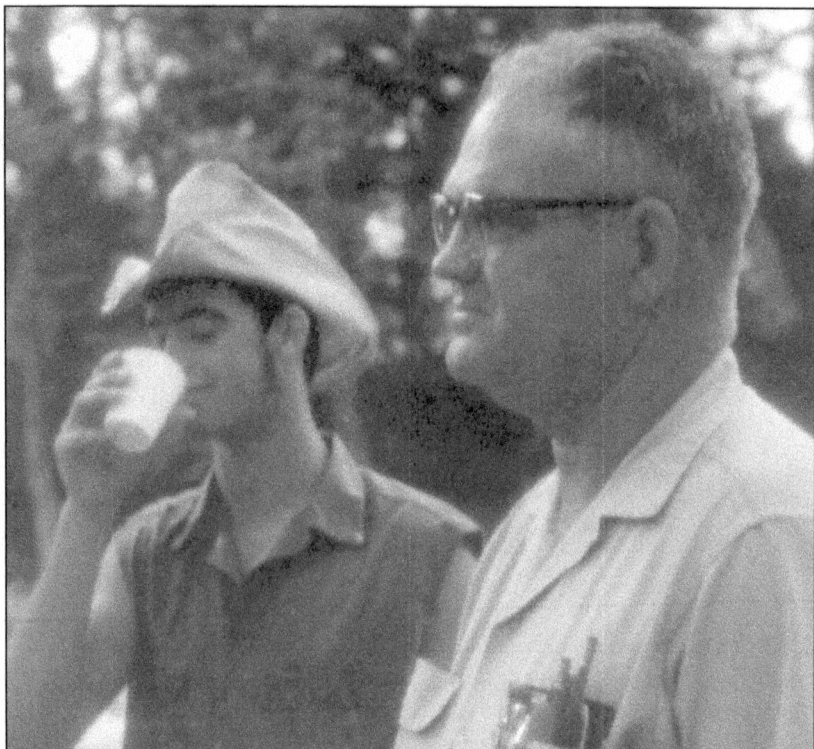

Don and his father, Jerry Durden, in champagne toast

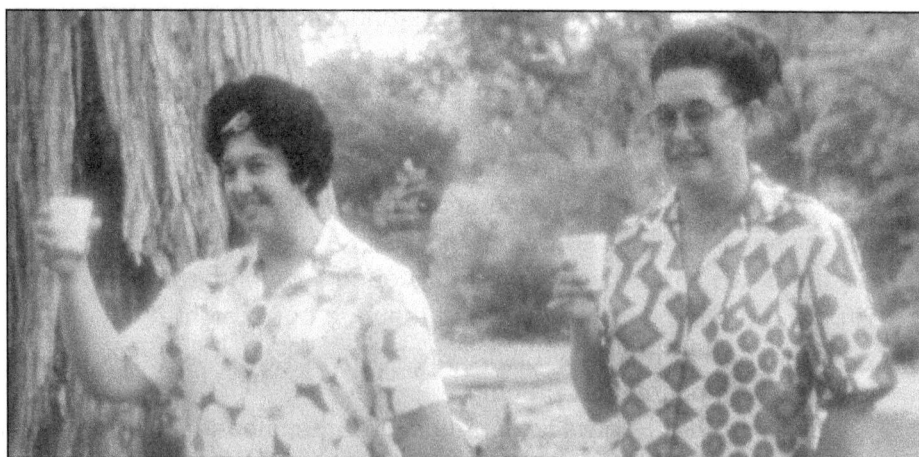

Nervous mothers, Mae Durden and Vera Rausch echo toast " to a safe and exciting journey…"

Little brother Roger Durden helps pull canoe out to water while James and Don Durden get ready.

James and Don Durden launch.

Peter Krauter and Mark Rausch ready to launch.

Peter and Mark paddle away.

Canoe trip
takes shape

After many months of thinking, planning, practicing and debating some more, four Comfort young men have decided to "do it!"

And, if all goes well at these last stages of gathering together equipment and grub, Donald Durden, seventeen year old son of Mr. and Mrs. Jerry Durden, Jr., James Durden, fifteen year old son of the Jerry Durden's; Mark Rausch, seventeen year old son of Mr. and Mrs. Hubert Rausch; and Peter Kreuter, fifteen year old son of Mr. and Mrs. James Kreuter, all of Comfort, will be leaving June 7, 1971 on a canoe expedition from Comfort to the Gulf Coast of Texas at the San Antonio Bay area.

The trip is estimated to be approximately 200 miles and the young men estimate that the trip will take from three to four weeks. The young men plan to be back in time for the July 4th Homecoming to celebrate.

The Comfort News *covers the story ... wrong date.*

The First Day on the River

From Don Durden's Journal—Monday, June 7, 1971:

"We left the Waring crossing exactly at 8:00 A.M. on schedule amid champagne toasts and good wishes. I felt no different than I had at any other departures ... no feelings of remorse at leaving the luxuries and conveniences of home ... no hints of the loneliness yet to come. No ideas at all of reaching the ultimate goal filled my consciousness ...

"James and I shared one canoe and Peter and Mark the other. The steep banks of the river are sometimes wild with brush. Other times, sandy beaches gently slope down to the water's edge. The smell of the river is not unfamiliar as ever since we were old enough—and whenever Mom would let us go—James and I had spent lots of time fishing and messing around the riverbanks. Peter and Mark too had practically grown up on the river so this environment was not new to them either.

"James and I are usually ahead of Pete and Mark. Not that we are in a race. It just seems that since I am the oldest—I should take leadership and it is more like follow the leader.

"We paddled without incident. About 11:40 A.M. we reached the Boerne/Sisterdale 1376 Road. Since we were in good spirits, without a break we ate lunch on the move. Lunch was fried chicken.

"We discussed our plans while we paddled along. Being that we were ahead of schedule and not too tired, we decided to move on for at least another 18 minutes or 11 miles to reach our first night's camp.

"Upon our arrival at our planned stopping place for our first night of this excursion, we were happy and surprisingly energetic. For this reason, the decision to continue on was unanimous. When we arrived at the Golden Fawn Guest Ranch, I went up to the office to ask permission to camp there overnight along the river. They were nice but said they could not allow us to stay. We simply took no for our answer and consulted our maps. One mile or thirty more minutes of paddling will take us to Camp Alzafar at RR 474. It was 7:35 P.M. when we set up camp there and ate some chicken soup.

"We walked a lot today. Portaging a loaded canoe is not easy work. Hopefully the water will increase as we continue down the river.

"The noteworthy event of our first day was the capture of a turtle. At the announcement of the capture of him or her—we couldn't tell the sex—we were faced with several courses of action. Mark, as a good humanitarian would, suggested that we keep him as our mascot and train him as a pet. James suggested we could have turtle soup. Fortunately for the turtle, we simply named him Moby Prick— and all had a good laugh! Somehow the turtle escaped during the night.

The turtle captured the first day. A mascot?

Getting ready for the first night out

Peter Krauter's Journal:

"My entire bedding consisted of two army blankets: one to lie on and one to lie under. This first night we plan to sleep on the rocky sandbar within the stream boundaries because we did not want to trespass on someone's property. We slept directly on the ground on the bank of the river.

"The river is trickling over the rocks, the crickets are singing, and everyone is laying ready to drift into deep sleep. The sun, fighting to cast its last rays over the earth, which we see, signals the end of a hard day in which we began our journey down the River Guadalupe. The actual test was today, when we found out everything anticipated was true. There are many hard times ahead of us …"

James Durden recalls:

"My first grim dose of reality came at bedtime that first night. They wanted to sleep on the ground. Not my first rodeo! I've fished this river before and it is difficult to find a nice smooth flat spot along the banks of the Guadalupe River in the Texas Hill Country.

"I'm not sure where the idea came from. I have to say now it was a formulation of some over-active thinking. The practicality of the situation did not equal the factors we used to derive the conclusion! Where those "factors" came from I have no idea—though I do seem to recollect that in one of our visits to the Army/Navy Surplus Store to get supplies for the trip that we spotted *hammocks* and decided (albeit too hastily) that hammocks would be a wonderful alternative to sleeping on the ground. Whether Bob Roberts was part of our decision-making, I do not recall. I don't think so. He may have given his "blessing" to the idea, but I submit that he only did that to get us out of his hair and onto the river. Anyway, to use a hammock you need trees! Okay. I had to abandon my plan to use my hammock this first night and I too started looking for a nice smooth flat spot on which to sleep."

Don, James, and Mark and the first night in camp.

No doubt talking about sleeping on the rocks!

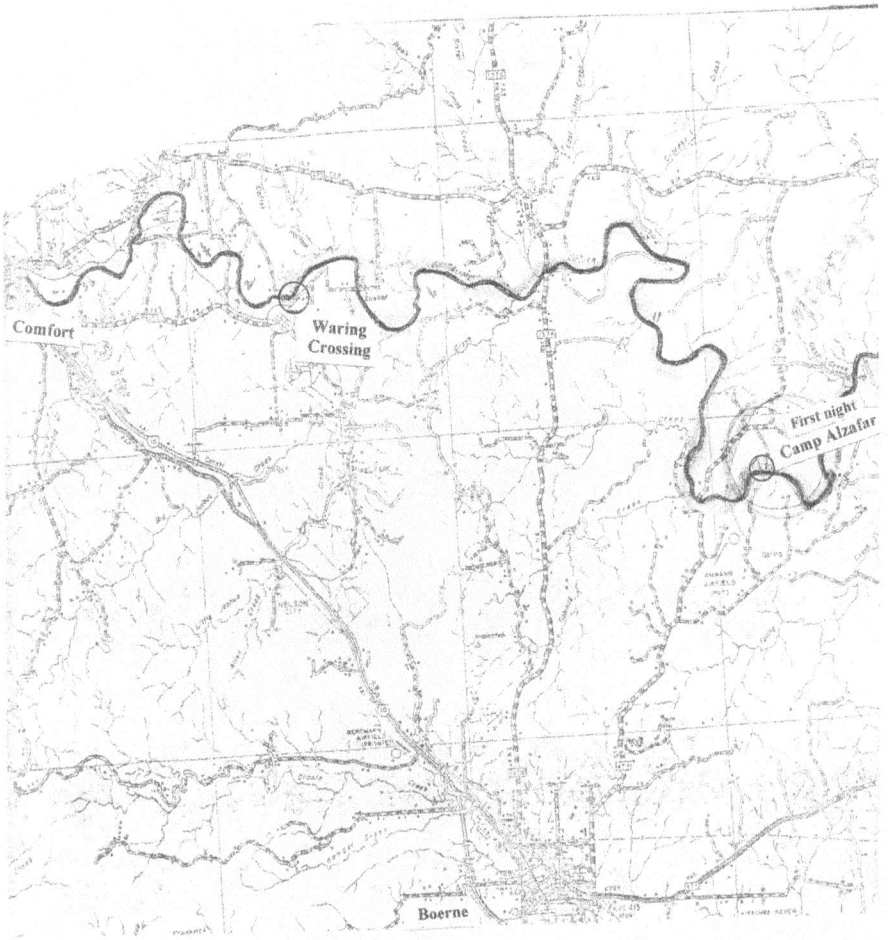

Map of first night

Day Two, June 8, Tuesday

Peter Krauter's Journal:

"After spending the night sleeping on river rocks on my army blanket, I felt a good amount of soreness this morning, and trespassing or not, decided to at least find a place in the future where there was soil to make my bed.

"We were up early—maybe because none of our beds were for sleeping late. Besides that, I think we were anxious to get started and back on the river.

"We had eggs for breakfast. They are powdered eggs mixed up with water ... supposed to taste like scrambled eggs. Not too bad.

"We have no assigned duties or routine to pack up to break camp. Everyone just pitches in. We shoved off at 7:40 to move on down the river toward our destination. The day seemed easier than the first, maybe because there were long stretches of water deep enough to paddle through and few rapids. After dinner, we were expecting to get to one bridge in about 4 miles, only to find it around the bend. This was a tremendous morale boost for it meant we were about 4 to 6 miles ahead of schedule. The river and its banks have gotten beautiful. After a tiring day, we camped on a ledge overlooking pretty, rocky rapids up river, high granite cliffs down river, and ready for a restful night of sleep."

From Don Durden ...

"The way I figured it, for a bunch of greenhorn canoers we were making fairly good time. The river is getting better. Not too many rapids. We did find however that as the number of rapids decreased, their intensity increased.

"We unexpectedly reached the crossing at 2:55 P.M.—not the calculated 3:45 P.M. By our figuring, and by the bends in the river, we should be about two miles into Comal County.

"This spot is the prettiest one yet. Of course, that's not too unusual considering that this is only the second night. The sun is almost down behind the cypress trees and the river makes little gurgling noises as it flows over a natural waterfall about four or five feet high. Down river from this pool is a mirror-like pond that we found to be about twelve to fourteen feet deep with a gravel bottom.

This is the prettiest spot so far ...

"We saw five artesian springs today and we filled our water canteens. We also went sixteen miles today before we saw another human being besides ourselves. Anyone who wants to get away from it all should come here. The water is clean and the beer cans are not too great in number.

"Tonight—rocks are rough sleeping place again! Not too good. Still no trees for our hammocks. Everyone sleeps on the ground. Coffee is good. We're low on bread. I just ate a can of peaches. Tomorrow is day three. I'm listening to the frogs and crickets as they seem to be arguing back and forth with each other trying to drown the others out with his own song. I should think that with all this around me that I should be satisfied … I'm still restless … must be the rocks!"

Map of second day

10

Day Three, June 9, Wednesday

Don's Journal:

"My mind and body are becoming accustomed to this life even though the rocks were hard again last night. Four people in constant contact with each other could get very bored with one another but this is not the case here! The only reason that I can see for the good moral is that we are coming near to one of the great challenges of our trip. We are now at the head of Canyon Lake Reservoir.

At the head waters of Canyon Lake, vultures are overhead! Is this an omen?

"We really got a lift this morning when we passed two other canoes at the Highway 281 crossing. They were four boys from Houston piloting canoes. Just as we had done, they too left from Comfort. The only difference was that they left there on June 5 and we had left on the seventh! We had seen their scrapings on rocks before we caught up to them.

"We also met two other boys this evening. We are very indebted to them. First, they gave us each a cold drink and then towed us to Crane's Mill Park, which is located on the Southwest shore of Canyon Lake off FM 2673 and is a state controlled area. Then, as if they had not done enough, they gave us a ride to a grocery store where we celebrated our being ahead of schedule by buying some jelly, sweet rolls, bread, soda water and other candy and sweets."

James Durden remembers:
"As we entered the upper reaches of Canyon Lake, the old river bed is marked by the dead tops of long ago drowned cy-

Dan and James ahead dwarfed by cypress trees

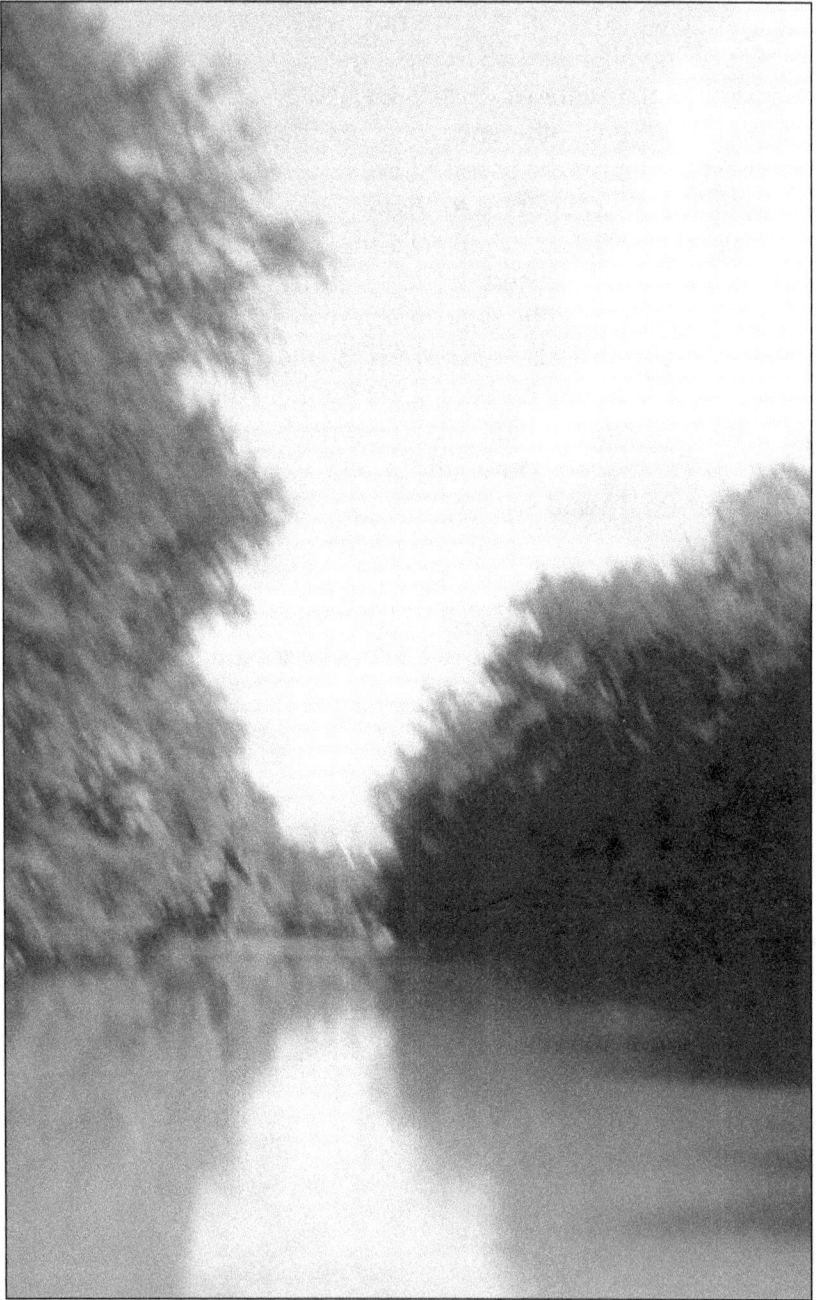

Stretch of deeper, somewhat murky water

Natural falls just above Spring Branch

Mark calls for a rest stop

Getting closer to the headwaters of Canyon Lake

High ridge overlooking lake headwaters

Some herons taking flight … we are almost there.

press trees covered by the rising waters of the lake. These gnarly barren old trees make it appear as if you had just entered a sea of trees—but they clearly define where it's safe to boat and where boats must use caution to avoid underwater obstacles. What they also do is confine most high-speed boat traffic to a very narrow channel ... *the same channel that we were in* trying to navigate our way into Canyon Lake. Naturally, we were a bit apprehensive about our first encounter with motorized boating. Would they be able to see us? Would they take a devilish delight in trying to swamp us? Would they pay heed to our greater vulnerability and avoid us? Would they even slow down to reduce their wake in our presence? All these questions were rolling through our heads as we formulated a plan for our first encounter.

"We decided that when the time came the best policy would be to err on the side of safety. Our plan was that when we'd hear an approaching boat, we would simply paddle to the nearest tree and hug onto the biggest limb we could find, cross our fingers, and hope for the best.

These gnarly barren old trees near the lake entrance make it appear as if you had just entered a sea of trees.

"When we heard the first boat—that's what we did. When it passed us it had slowed down to practically a crawl and all that we felt was a very gentle rocking of the canoe as their wake met the side of our canoes. Imagine how silly we felt! We must have looked like a bunch of sissies! After that encounter, we braved up considerably and actually started to enjoy the added thrill of a motorboat's wakes.

"We were lucky to receive a tow in the headwaters of Canyon Lake. Our apprehensive approach to power boats, and our slow progress trying to find our way along the main channel of the upper river, put us in a situation where night was going to fall before we made it to Cranes Mill Park, our planned destination for that evening. For that reason, when asked by a concerned boater if we wanted a tow, we decided it would be best to accept it as opposed to getting caught on the open lake after sundown.

"To get prepared for the tow, we lashed the two canoes together side by side to give us stability. As the motor boat began to tow us, the water was effectively trapped between our two canoe bows and as the boat went faster and faster, the height of the water between the canoes rose until it breeched the side of our canoes and we began to flood. It was time for some quick redesign!

"We discussed our problem and came up with this plan. We again lashed the canoes together but with a paddle's length between us. That solved the problem and we were able to make the tow all the way to the park. Some time later on in the trip it was implied that we had gotten a tow all the way through Canyon Lake. The answer is no! The day of the tow, we were still essentially still in the river. In any event, I would like to acknowledge the helpful nature of the fellow that gave us the tow and say, "Thanks for the assist.""

Another word from Don's journal:
"Tonight we are truly excited about tomorrow's challenge. Beginning in the morning, we must conquer Canyon Lake. For

some reason, tonight I am going back over one of my early childhood memories of a Sunday afternoon drive back in 1959 or 1960 with my family to go see Canyon Dam. It was under construction at the time of our visit and I guess Dad thought his boys would like to see the massive construction operation.

"I remember I was more impressed that Dad took us on a road trip than I was with the construction project. My dad worked all his adult life for Southwestern Engineering Company, for a company that designed telephone systems for rural telephone cooperatives, mostly in Texas. At that time in his career, Dad's work required that he leave home Sunday afternoon or evening and drive to the location of his current engagement. He would stay there all week; living out of a suitcase and eating in greasy spoon cafes, until Friday afternoon or night, when he would drive back home.

"Growing up, I didn't consider this a hardship or deficiency—it was just the way things were. It was what was needed to provide food and shelter for our family. Although my father was not a demonstrative man and I don't recall him telling me he loved me or missed his family, but I was confident that he did and I treasured spending time with him. (As Dad's tenure with telephone engineering company increased, he was eventually promoted to Vice President of the Outside Plant Division, and was able to spend more time at home.)

"Construction on the Canyon Dam project took about 5 years. An earthen dam—6,830 feet long—measured from the original river bank—is 224 feet high. The upstream face of the dam was covered by a several foot thick layer of large angular rock and boulders called rock rubble rip-rap. This covering, Dad explained, would prevent wave action from eroding the sloping bank which rises at a rate of about one foot for every two or three feet in horizontal distance. The down stream face slopes downward at about the same slope.

"Dad also talked about how this dam would eventually form a lake that would completely change this entire area. Who would have guessed—that long-ago Sunday afternoon—that little more than a decade later, my brother, two friends and I would find ourselves at the upstream end of Canyon Lake, pondering the best way to cross it in a canoe!

"It took all four of us a long time to get to sleep tonight …"

Map of Day Three

11

Day Four, June 10, Thursday

Canyon Lake

Don's Journal:

"The sun seemed to come up early this morning and there was a stiff northeastern breeze blowing across the lake. The first thing that happened this morning was that I ruined a batch of powdered eggs by adding too much water. Was I preoccupied? Probably. Anyway, instead of eggs, we drank cokes and ate sweet rolls for breakfast. As we ate, we talked about our options.

"The shortest route would be around the peninsula that is Cranes Mill Park and then head straight for the dam. That was probably also the riskiest. We could see whitecaps out on the lake and we wondered how our supply laden canoes would respond. If we were swamped, we knew our canoes' flotation would keep them from sinking to the bottom of the lake, but we were not sure about our gear and frankly about ourselves. (*We did not carry life jackets.*) Even if everything stayed afloat, it would be extremely difficult, if not impossible to right a canoe in the middle of the lake.

"Another choice would be to hug the shoreline as closely as possible, so that in the event we were swamped, we could easily retrieve our gear and right the canoe and continue. The problem with this approach was that it would probably make our trip to the dam more than three times longer than the direct approach.

"Another aspect of our deliberation dealt with which side of the lake we should follow, the north shore or the south shore. Rightly or wrongly, we reasoned that the north shore was somewhat more protected from the northeast wind than the south shore, and therefore it wouldn't be as rough. We decided to postpone the final decision about our route to the dam until we tested how bad it was to cross the lake to get to the north side.

"We broke camp. It did not take us long to pack up and we headed out in our canoes.

"We took off along the shore line of Cranes Mill Park. As we left the cover provided by the park peninsula and entered the open water of the lake, the wind and waves became a significant factor. Now, headed almost directly into the wind, it was difficult to tell if we were making any progress at all, and the waves required that we frequently bail water from our canoes.

Daybreak at Cranes Mill Park ... we could see white caps out on the lake. Not a good thing.

"Ever so slowly we moved across the lake. It would not be accurate to say that we were comfortable with the roughness of the lake, because we were far from it. *We were scared!* We were however learning about how to better cope with the circumstances. James and Mark, who were in the bows of the canoes, learned that if they timed their strokes so the blades of their paddles entered the water just before the canoe encountered a wave, they could slightly lift the front of the canoe and minimize the amount of water that came in over the gunnels. However, in order to do this they had to reach out in front to the bow of the canoe and exert more of a downward force on the paddle than a backward force. This took a lot more work than normal paddling and they were exhausted by the time we finally reached the north shore. We beached the canoes and evaluated our situation again.

"To the southeast across a cove lay Potters Creek Park. The distance looked to be somewhat longer than the open water we had just crossed, but hugging the shoreline we estimated would take three to four times as long. We figured the crossing would simply be more of the same thing we had just done.

"We made our decision and took off across the open water headed for Potters Creek Park. Our speculation had proven correct and we made that crossing without incident and proceeded along the south shore of Potters Creek Park.

"Once more we stopped to study our situation. We saw now a tract of private land and beyond that laid another stretch of open water, with Jacobs Creek Park on the other side. This stretch of open water looked to be almost twice as wide as the two we had just crossed and again we considered a meandering route closer to the shoreline. We rejected that route as too time-consuming. *We wanted to get off this windy, rough lake as soon as possible* and if it meant taking a little riskier route, well, that was okay. We promised ourselves we would reward ourselves with a snack at Jacob's Creek Park and we took off.

"A little less than an hour of paddling and we were across the open water and moving southeast along the shoreline of Jacobs

James observing the windy conditions on the lake from Potter's Creek Park.

This photo shot at the water level at Potter's Creek Park did nothing to lessen our worries about the wind.

Creek Park. We looked for a place to beach for our snack. Maybe the conversation about where to stop distracted us or perhaps it was an unusually large wave or maybe it came from a different direction. Whatever it was happened so fast that I didn't realize what was going on until our canoe was full of water right up to the gunnels. James and I both rolled out of the canoe and fortunately found solid bottom beneath our feet. The shallow water swamping answered the debate about where to stop for a snack, and we pulled our partially submerged canoe toward the shore, herding floating tins, trash bags full of bedding, and other flotsam as we went. Mark and Peter did not suffer the same ordeal with their canoe.

"We emptied our canoe of the rest of the gear, righted it, and pulled in up on the shore. Then we checked the tins holding our food and the bags with our bedding for leaks. Fortunately, everything was okay and we enjoyed a snack of canned peaches and bread as we rested up for the next challenge.

"We now had one more stretch of open water to cross. We had been lucky that the swamping had occurred in relatively shallow water. We were now keenly aware of just *how fast* we could be swamped and how truly difficult it would be to come away from a deep water swamping with all our gear intact, perhaps even with our very lives.

"But, even though the swamping was fresh in our minds, we took off and about an hour later we were relieved to be past the last of the open water crossings.

"As we now slowly approached the dam, we realized that this was no little pile of dirt. We scanned the upstream face of the dam for some sort of access road, but alas, none was visible. We pulled up to the face and did our best to secure the canoes to the large rocks.

"The water level was low and the climb to the top of the dam, approximately eighty feet above the water, was difficult. It was hard to find good footing on the large rocks and the slope was steeper than it looked.

"At first, we tried to portage the canoes fully loaded with our

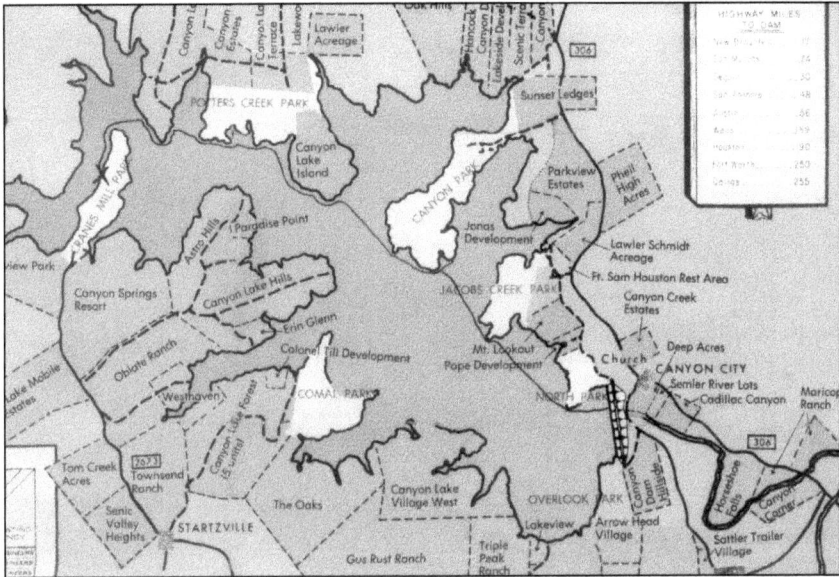

This reduced map of the entire Canyon Lake shows a fine line drawing of the route the canoes took to the dam.

Heading straight for the dam ... Mark is paddling.

Above: *Getting closer to the dam and safety*

Below: *We stopped to rest looking back over Canyon Lake, reflecting on the experience in silence.*

gear, but they were too heavy for the difficulty of the climb. So, we began making trips to the top of the dam, carrying as much of our gear as we could and staging it there. This required three round trips—two for the gear and one for the canoes. By the time we got everything moved, we were totally exhausted.

"We stopped to rest then, looking back over Canyon Lake, reflecting on the experience in silence, taking some pictures, and slowing shifting our focus from where we had been to where we needed to go."

From James Durden:

Crossing Canyon Lake with small craft advisories out

"When we woke up in this morning we could tell it was not going to be a good day. The sky was overcast and there was a strong wind blowing from southeast to northwest. Canyon Lake was a great gray mass of water and it was churning heavily from the wind. We had examined our maps the night before and had made the decision that in order to expedite our passage through

the lake we would need to somehow get to the *north* shore and follow it around to the dam. We had decided that rather than follow right along the shoreline—to lessen those many miles— we would attempt to go from point to point. The north shoreline was by far the shorter due to the small nature of its inlets and bays that the lake had formed as it filled. The only problem was, starting out this morning, we are on the *south* shore. We've got to get to the north shore.

"Under gray cloudy skies, in a high wind, and with the lake showing white caps, our first task would have to be somehow to get across the lake to the north shore. Naturally, at first we were very pleased to see no motor boat traffic on the lake. Our canoes—even with two occupants—made for a very low visibility, low profile object. And, having only paddle power, we were not able to move very quickly *were we to spot a boat that had not spotted us first*. So, we always felt vulnerable and insecure. Not seeing any boats lifted a huge burden. Nevertheless, that didn't get us to the other shore …

"As we paddled out into the lake, we soon discovered a rhythm of paddling. We allowed the canoe to lift on the rising wave, and then, just as the bow broke free from the wave, a paddle stroke would shoot us out into the valley between the waves allowing us to make forward progress while only taking on a small amount of water. Of course, because of the length of the crossing even this small amount of water soon became problematic. Bob Roberts had shown us how to use gallon Clorox bottles—the lids on tight and the bottoms cut off—as lightweight bails to keep the canoe free from water. But, the amount of water that was coming in over and around the bow from the waves was soon getting way ahead of what Don was able to bail. He soon had to abandon his paddling and spent most of his time bailing while I tried to keep us moving forward toward our destination.

"We finally reached the north bank and Don and I were paddling along the shoreline. Remember I mentioned the wind was from the southeast? Well, that meant that while we were crossing the lake the waves had been running in the same direction as the canoe and they were hitting us from the right rear or along the longitudinal axis of the canoe. Once we turned to the east, the waves began hitting us broadside from the starboard side of the canoe after running across the full width of the lake.

"We couldn't have been more than thirteen feet from the shore—when a gigantic wave rolled in—right over the top of us and completely filled the canoe with water and it sat right down on the bottom of the lake! Now I don't remember for sure where this event happened—but I think it was possibly one cove (or point) east of where we crossed. I just remember it happened right after we crossed. In any event, when it happened, I know it rattled me! Don and I just sat there—canoe full of water—completely grounded—soaking wet—thinking, *what the hell are we doing here?*

"Peter and Mark came up behind us and suggested we break for lunch! We agreed. We unpacked the canoe—bailed her out—and pulled it up on the bank. We *had* reached the north shore and we were all thankful, tired, and *probably ten years older.*"

"I was a lot more apprehensive when we took off again after lunch. We had managed to reason through the swamping and realized that it was only because we were in such shallow water so close to the shore that this wave had swamped us.

"Happily, the rest of the crossing was not only uneventful, but like so many things that happened on this trip, done with ease and a sense of style and grace that made us look like we were seasoned professionals. I will say this for us: We learned to adapt quickly. When we ran up against an obstacle, together we figured out how to overcome it. Sometimes it took a few hard lessons but we always managed to get through it.

"When we finally reached the face of the dam at Canyon Lake everyone was pretty tired and relieved. Not only had we crossed Canyon Lake and traversed its full length under *paddle power* but also we had done it under small craft advisories that had kept other boats at the pier. We were proud of that. The problem that faced us now: How do we get over the dam?

When we finally reached the face of Canyon Dam we were tired but proud that we had traversed its full length under paddle power—even with small craft warning advisories that thankfully kept other boats at the pier.

"The face of Canyon Dam is nothing but huge broken rock unimaginably difficult to walk on—much less carry a loaded canoe over them. It soon became obvious if we were going to go up and over it would have to be with empty canoes. So, we began packing all the cargo up the face of the dam to the road on top. This took several trips per canoe for everyone—and let me tell you, Canyon Dam is not a small dam. Combining the steepness of the dam with the burden of the cargo and the difficulty of the rock and the fact that we had already paddled across Canyon Lake under adverse conditions—by the time we got everything to the road on top of the dam—we were just plain pooped out! But, if we thought the climb up the rocky face was difficult—it was just a precursor for what lay ahead!

"The back side of Canyon Dam is covered with dirt and coastal Bermuda grass. There are two terraces that run the length of the dam at approximately one-third and two-thirds the height of the dam to prevent erosion on the backside. Truth is

View of the gate superstructure at the dam

that *it's a long way down* to the county road located immediately below the dam.

"Faced with the prospect of having to now carry all the cargo to the bottom of the dam and then hike back up to get the canoes was just more then we could fathom. We discussed our dilemma and we decided to load up the canoes with all our stuff and then attempt to slide them down the grassy slope with ropes thereby making the trip all at one time with no need to climb back up to the top. *Ingenious!*

"We tied everything into the canoes then secured tag lines on to the front and rear of the canoes and, holding tension on the tag lines, we nudged the canoes over the edge of the downhill slope.

"I don't recall how far we made it before the weight and momentum of the loaded canoes overcame us. Seems like almost *immediately* the canoes took off like bullets heading downhill with an ever-growing velocity. I tried to hold on to my rope! Lord knows I tried! While everyone else abandoned the canoes to their fate, I doggedly held on—I ended up being pulled off my

The view of the backside from the top and valley below dam.

feet and onto my butt and being pulled down hill by our canoe until it came to rest on the first of the two terraces!

"My butt end was okay but my pride suffered tremendously. After we inspected the canoes for damage, discovered none, we decided to do it all over again and sent the canoes over this terrace to the next one below.

"The worst slide turned out to be the last one—from the lowest terrace to the roadway. The barrow ditch located between the dam and the road is deep, and the canoes literally crashed into the side against the road. It was a miracle that neither canoe sustained any damage. The bigger miracle—we had managed to get the canoes to the bottom of Canyon Dam!

"Having arrived at the bottom of the dam, each crew now picked up their canoe and we proudly walked across the road to the discharge channel. A Corp of Engineers employee was there

inspecting the discharge channel or checking out this or that and I remember the surprised look on his face as we came walking up carrying our two canoes. *He had to have known from our appearance that we* hadn't just been dropped off at the road. Also, we had seen the **Keep Off The Dam** signs *everywhere and our guilty faces must have been a sight to behold.* But, he never said a word. He just watched us set our canoes in the river and we took off."

The Gospel of the Dam according to Don:

"Finally, we had everything to the top of the dam. Now we had to make a decision on how to descend to the foot of the dam. In the end, we agreed that the fastest way was to pack our gear back into the canoes was to tie a rope to each one and then just let them slide down the grassy slope of the dam itself. We didn't know how difficult that would be! We didn't count on the canoes being so heavy and that they would slide so fast. We fell down a lot and slid and James busted his butt pretty good one time.

"When we finally got to the foot of the dam we looked back up the grassy slope. There were two deep trenches made by our two canoes! Also, a Corp of Engineer person was waiting for us. *'Where did you boys come from?'* When we told him where we had come from and where we were still going, he let us go on with a lecture on just how dangerous our idea had been.

"When we finally got back on the river in our canoes, it was about 2:00 P.M. We went on a little further down river, changed clothes, and went to eat out at the Dam Site Cafe. Everybody ate a 10 oz. steak. Man! That was good! We also called our parents to tell them we'd crossed the lake safely and to bring more food supplies when they came to meet us on Sunday.

"After lunch we returned to our canoes and continued on down the river. We had to go over four more small 2 to 4 foot unmarked dams, had to cross roads twice, and went about a mile or two before we stopped for the night. It was 6:30 P.M. We ate ranch style beans and peaches. James wants it recorded that he and Mark washed the dishes. Peter's gone fishing. No luck so far. We camped out at somebody's pretty picnic ground."

Peter's rather short journal records:

"Had unusual and exciting experience going through Canyon Lake. Wind was strong and made waves to complicate traveling. *Found it easier than expected going over dam.* In river below dam, water was around 40°F, clear, and sparsely populated with trout. River is running back into more abrupt canyons. Being around a day ahead of schedule, there's a feeling of accomplishment, but still the responsibility of pushing on and making time till the end is reached."

Final comment from Don's Journal:

"We are unbelievably tired. What a day! What an experience."

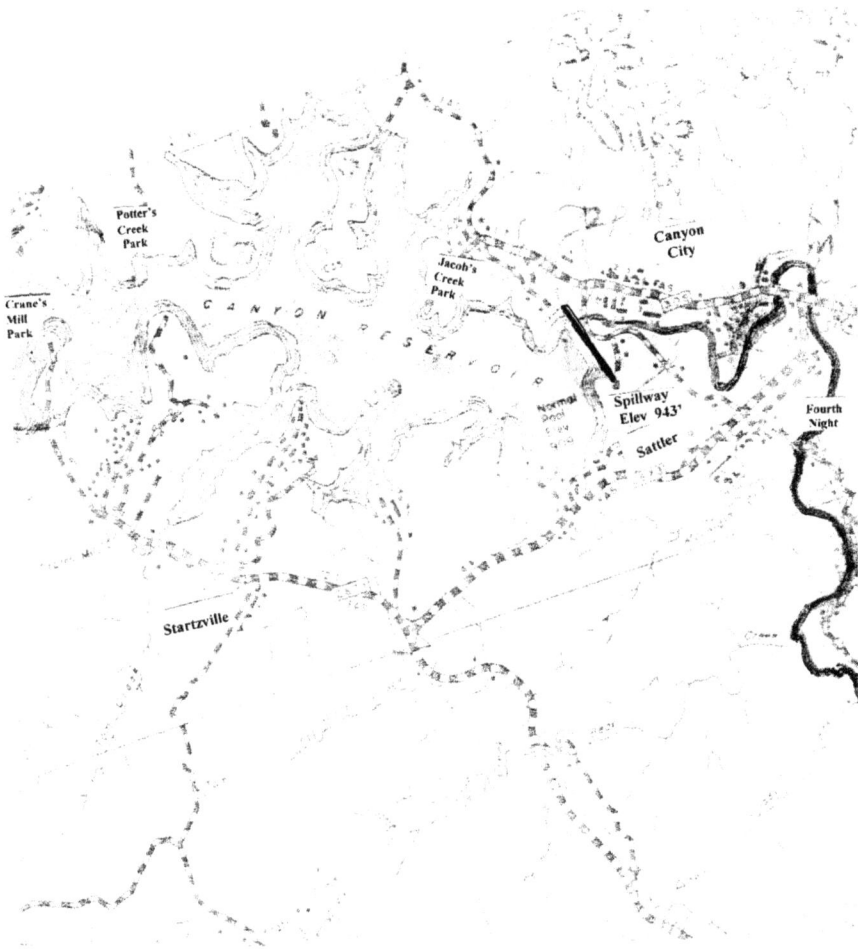

Map of Day Four

Day Five, June 11, Friday

From Peter's Journal:

"At daybreak, the chinking sound of small rocks hitting each other woke me, and without moving, I opened my eyes to discover a doe cautiously making her way down the steep hill across the river to drink water. I lay motionless and watched as she drank her fill before beginning the long climb back up the steep hill away from the river. It was a peaceful experience that I will never forget."

From Don's Journal:

"We started our day around 7:20 A.M. and canoed about average. There was lots of shallow water with rocks. Some places we had to go back and forth across the river so we didn't make too good of time. We ate hamburgers and a sausage for lunch at K&L Tavern; really nice people there. We went on through New Braunfels until we got to IH-35. I think there we walked up and ate Lemburgers. Now all except $3.00 of our money was gone. Called home again. "Bring money!""

Again from Peter's journal:

"After a hard day of trying to reach a minor goal, New

60

Braunfels, we finally got to town and ate at a hamburger stand. Since Randolph Bohnert, a friend of ours—formerly of Comfort—now lives here, we contacted him and he came and picked us up for a night of relaxation and rest in his air-conditioned house on a canyon overlooking the city."

Nice bluffs overlooking river below Canyon Dam

Horseshoe Falls below Canyon Dam

Map of Day Five

Day Six, June 12, Saturday

Don Durden Journal:

"We hit the river around 7:20 A.M. this morning as we wanted to make good time today so we can rest on Sunday. We went over Dunlap (no whirlpools). We went through McQueeny, and picked up a tow to the dam about 2 to 3 miles away. At Lake Placid, like all the others there was a gate to release water and an electric plant. We had to portage around both of these. This took about 20-30 minutes for each portage. Meadow Lake was the same but worse because we were so tired. About 300 yards from Meadow Lake Dam we hit Highway 466, our stopping place. Now we can rest until our parents get here on Sunday. We ate chicken again for supper—bland but okay. We are looking forward to our parents visit tomorrow. We are all wishing we had told them to come earlier. Our water is tasting bad."

James recalls the day's events somewhat differently:

All the lakes below New Braunfels

"Once we overcame the mighty Canyon Lake it seemed as if there wouldn't be anything more to impede our progress down

63

the river. Little did we know that our Canyon Dam experience was to become a fond memory as we progressed onward towards the coast. I'm not sure I can recall the names of all the lakes or all the dams. But it seems like once we got beyond New Braunfels, all we did was portage around one dam after another: Lake Placid, Lake Wood, Lake McQueeney, Lake Dunlop, Lake Nolte, and Lake Gonzales, and countless other lakes and less majestic dams abandoned in-place years ago by the GBRA. Some of the lakes were only wide straight spots in the river while others were mazes of inlets and islands with no clearly defined channel. By far the most serious misadventure involved the dam bypass canal associated with Lake Dunlop.

"As we crossed Dunlop, we noticed that there was a relatively wide, concrete lined canal that extended past the left side of the dam and appeared (according to our maps) to reenter the

Lily-covered Lake Dunlop

river some distance below the dam. Maybe it was in desperation or just plain lack of forethought, but we decided, *if taking the canal got us out of having to portage over yet another dam*, it was worth a try. So, off we went, paddling down the canal. We had no idea—and there sure was no signage indicating the canal was **not for boat use**!

"We paddled on and on and on only stopping occasionally to discuss whether we had made the right decision or not. At some point it actually seemed like the current in the canal was running against us but I'm sure it was simply fatigue and worry starting to get the better of us. We finally rounded a bend in the channel and spotted what looked like the end of the canal! *A large structure straddled the canal.* We could also see a large metal lined opening just below it at water level. We gingerly paddled up to the metal gate that held back the water in the canal and I looked over the gate. I could just faintly see the riverbed below us —*about 150 feet below us—and straight down below us at that!*

"I made some desperate remarks about the need to *get the hell away from the gate* and started frantically back paddling—certain that the gate was fixing to open at any moment. I told Don what I had seen and we paddled back up the canal about 100 yards before stopping to discuss what I had observed. We were worried—*as well we should have been!* If they'd opened the gate while we were in the canal, we'd be sucked through the narrow slit below the powerhouse and the canoes would be destroyed not to mention our own possible loss of life.

"There was a quick discussion and we concluded that the time necessary to paddle back to the lake would only increase our risk of being caught in a release. So, it was decided that we would abandon the canal and portage around the power house and down the 150 feet or so to the original river bed below.

"The first major task then was to *get ourselves and the canoes out of that canal.* The water level in the canal was about five feet below the top of the side walls and if you've ever tried to stand up in a canoe and jump up onto a concrete ledge five feet above you, you can understand that just getting ourselves out of the canal was no easy task!

"After numerous attempts, we finally succeeded and managed to set up a rope line to assist us. We unloaded the canoes and using ropes and brute force, we managed to drag the canoes up the side of the canal and onto the bank between the canal and the riverbed. From here, we reloaded the canoes and started the arduous task of lowering the canoes down the nearly straight down embankment to the riverbed below. This embankment was mostly riprap consisting of huge boulders. As we moved the canoes along over them, I remember seeing many long curly spirals of aluminum off our canoe bottoms—scratched by the sharp jagged rocks.

"Once we reached the original riverbed, we paddled off down river determined to put as much distance as possible between us and the Lake Dunlop Powerhouse."

James also recalls

Difficulties and unrest in their paradise adventure
Peter and Mark's difficulties with rapids

"I hesitate to talk about this since it probably won't sound too flattering for either of them but Peter and Mark began to have some real issues when it came to canoe handling in the limited rapids of the Guadalupe River.

"Don and I had gotten a lot of practice boat handling when we were growing up and spending lots of time fishing the Guadalupe River around Comfort. While all that was primarily done in a jonboat the principals were pretty much the same for the canoes we had on this trip. That plus the fact that Don is an excellent helmsman when it comes to steering and he thinks and responds quickly to rapidly changing conditions such as exist when running rapids. He and I developed a very good sense of what we could and could not do with our canoe and actually enjoyed shooting rapids whenever we could. We maneuvered our canoe with exceptional teamwork and a cooperative spirit that maybe can only exist between brothers. Mark and Peter were not quite so well oiled as a team— at least not right at first.

"Typically, Don and I were slightly ahead of Peter and Mark but let me state right here and now for the record—this was never a race! Far from it. We just seemed to make slightly better time then Mark and Peter and we were therefore usually ahead of them. This meant we got to rapids before they did and had to analyze them and proceed for better or worse. Once we got through a rapid, we would pull over below them so we could regroup with Mark and Peter before setting off on the next stretch of river. Frequently we would hear Mark yelling at Peter or Peter yelling at Mark to do this or do that or stop doing this or stop doing that and pretty soon, here would come the bags with the cargo from their canoe floating down the river. We'd get out of our canoe, grab the stuff, and throw it out on the gravel until Mark and Peter and the overturned canoe arrived. Naturally, there was always a lot of blame and name-calling going on regarding who was at fault. We'd help them reload and off we'd go again just to repeat the scene below the next set of rapids.

"It was not long before they got into a pretty heated argument which led to a wrestling match. We quickly decided in the best interest of the group to split them up. I remember Don and I switched, he went with Peter or Mark and I went with the other for a day to give them a break from each other. Today I don't remember who I was with (I guess it helps when you are only a bowman and don't have to look at someone's back all day!) but our strategy must have worked because after one day we were all back with our normal partners and it stayed that way until the end of the trip."

"By the end of the trip, Peter and Mark were as good as any canoeist team anywhere but those first few days were rough on them. If nothing else, I have to applaud them for sticking with it! Many people would have given up. They didn't.

Peter's journal of that day:
"Today started out as a hard day, turned into a hard day,

and ended a hard day, everyone is tired and touchy. Tomorrow, since we made double time today in order to get to Highway 466, where our parents are going to visit us, we aren't going to even move the canoes.

"Today, we crossed, actually we carried the canoes across, four dams which were hell to get over. Skin tans are getting dark, on two of us anyway, and we're beginning to look like Latinos. But, other than all of this, everybody is looking forward to talking to someone we know, even if they're our parents. I am anticipating a sense of assurance on the rest of our trip.

"It was probably due to fatigue and the need to vent a little steam, but there was a disagreement that came up between Mark and me that led to a little good-natured wrestling. While I don't remember taking it at all serious, Mark started to get upset, and Donald interceded verbally, at which point I backed-off and let Mark calm down. Between comrades in the journey, it was quickly forgotten."

Another vignette from James:

The smell of watermelons —

"This was probably a phenomenon created as much in our minds as anything but once it seemed like all we could ever smell along the river was watermelons. Maybe it was our diet— or the fact that watermelons always represented something good and refreshing—or maybe it was simply because we could almost never see beyond the immediate banks of the river—but the smell of watermelons seemed to follow us or proceed us everywhere we went. Finally, the urge to get one of those dang *watermelons* finally proved too great and one day Don had us land the canoes and he climbed the bank and went on a watermelon-finding mission.

"Meanwhile Peter, Mark, and I rested. Don returned sometime later empty handed without *ever* even spotting a watermelon patch—*or at least that's what he claimed*. After that we all concluded that while deserts have their mirages of water and shade laden oasis, it in no way compares to the watermelon mirage that existed along the mighty Guadalupe River."

Map of Day Six

14

Day Seven, June 13, Sunday

On our first prearranged parent rendezvous

James remembers

"Before we left on this canoe trip we had worked out a re-supply strategy with our parents. Based on an estimated amount of river that we could cover in a day, we had established several road crossing sites along the river where we would meet, spend the day resting, and take on the supply of food and dry clothing before moving on down the river. Of course, we really didn't have a good feel for how many miles we could cover in a day in a canoe since we had limited experience to fall back on. This, plus the fact that road crossings become fewer and fewer as the river drops out of the Hill Country, all added up—well—to us somehow missing our first rendezvous with our parents.

"As stated earlier, in preparation for our trip, Dad had secured copies of county maps for all the counties that the Guadalupe River travels through between Waring and the coast. We had laid out each day's estimated progress and determined basically where we would spend each night. This gave us a good measuring stick to gauge our progress as we traveled down the river so that we could time our arrival at the pre-determined re-supply crossings to coincide with the pre-determined schedule. Sounds like a good plan? Well, like my dad always said, even a poor plan is better than no plan at all. As it turned out, at least for the first rendezvous, it was bad!

"This is how it went: We actually made it to the first re-supply crossing a good day ahead of schedule. We debated then about waiting there for our parents to arrive but I suppose the teenager's necessity of always being on the move overcame us. We assumed that when our parents discovered we weren't at the prescribed crossing, they would simply work their way down-river following us until they found us. Therefore, we pushed on. Only problem was, *how were they to know we had already made the crossing?* How did they know we're pushing on and not just behind schedule and struggling to make it that far. *The thought never even crossed our minds that they would think that we might be **behind** schedule! Duh!*

"But that's exactly what happened. Sadly, this was long before the day of cellular telephones or wireless communications. Our parents pulled up to the X crossing expecting to find their sons all safe and sound and anxious to meet them. Instead, they found nothing! Not a situation teenagers should ever put their mom in, that's for sure, much less their dad! I'm surmising, but I suspect there were images of drowned boys brewing in their minds—plus internal questions as to how they could have ever agreed to this trip in the first place.

"But somehow their wiser and cooler heads prevailed. They ended up finding us where we were waiting at the Hwy 466 crossing. In retrospect, I am surprised they let us continue our trip.

"After discussing what had happened, we came up with an ingenious plan to signify our position on the river. From this point on, when we passed a road crossing, we would find a prominent limb or stump in the water and tie orange plastic survey marking tape to it. Then, should something happen, our parents would at least be able to look at each crossing and say, yes, they've been here or no, they haven't."

James Durden greets long over-due parents.

Boys have lots of explaining to do … need a better plan to meet.

Meanwhile, while waiting for parent' arrival

Again, from James:

"It's amazing just how filthy a canoe can get. You'd think if you were traveling in a canoe—in the water—that the canoe would stay relatively clean. This is just not so! Between runnings under low hanging limbs in the rapids, to climbing in and out to make portages, to the constant infusion of river water from paddles and wet clothes, our canoes ended up completely filthy by the end of the first week. So, being the *fastidious adventurers that we were*, we decided that while waiting for our parent's visit that first weekend, we would get the canoes in ship shape.

"We unloaded the canoes completely and armed only with paddles headed up river a short ways so we could make a *dash* to the camp location. Once we were alongside the campsite, under full paddle power, we would lean sideways in the canoe and cause it to roll and either capsize or take on enough water so we could wash out the canoe.

"Yep, we *had* a plan. And even though Don and I had never capsized or upset our canoe we assumed it must happen easy enough because Mark and Peter were doing it so often! Surely if they could do it, we could too!

"Okay—so here we go. Don and I both paddled like crazy in a frenzied sprint to build up as much speed as possible. As we near the campsite, Don yells, "One—Two—Three—LEAN!" Don leans left. I lean right! We both fall out of the canoe and the canoe kept right on going straight down the river! Mark and Peter retrieved our canoe and had a good laugh—*a really good laugh.*

"To save face, Don and I try again. This time we really do have a plan—same as before—but this time we will both lean right! Okay, get set, another hard paddling sprint to the campsite. One…Two…Three! LEAN! We both lean right grabbing the left side of the canoe as we go! The canoe begins to roll to the right, takes on a small amount of water, and then rights herself back on her keel as we both fall from the canoe once again! Mark and Peter are ready for this one. They are waiting down river—laughing more than ever.

"They finally bring our stubborn and stable canoe back to us. At this point, both Don and I have had enough. We grabbed the canoe and pressed her side down allowing water to rush into her hold. She filled with water, and sank down till only her prow and stern tips are showing above the water. But she never capsized! Seems Grumman canoes are virtually unsinkable.

"We finally got our canoe washed out and cleaned up and beached her next to our camp site. I don't think I recall ever seeing her looking prettier!"

A recollection from Peter on that Sunday:
"It was the sun's job to get us up this morning, for everybody slept until the brightness was too intense. No one wasn't bored, because there was absolutely nothing to do. Parents finally found us about 2:30 and it was wonderful talking to someone we know and hearing of home."

"That first week we suffered a number of ailments from sun and water exposure. As opposed to today when there are all sorts of specialized clothing for outdoor sports, we primarily wore cut-off jeans or army fatigues—except for Mark who somehow survived with regular jeans. We also wore old shirts with the sleeves cut off—again, except for Mark who wore either a t-shirt or sweatshirt. As a result, we were very overexposed to the sun, which was also reflected off the shiny bow and stern of the canoes. While we all incurred sunburn to varying degrees, James had a nasty looking blister about the size of a quarter in diameter, about $3/16$ths high, and filled with a greenish-yellowish pus on the back of his right shoulder. It wouldn't surprise me if he still has a visible scar from it today.

"I personally suffered from the effects of wet jeans and frequent portages through shallow stretches of river resulting in the worst case of chafed crotch imaginable. I recall describing my malady to my mother when we called to set up the Sunday rendezvous. She brought me this nasty smelling product called Foilles Ointment that remedied my situation. The ditching of my underwear also probably helped a great deal!"

The Meeting according to the parents:
"We finally found our kids around lunchtime and we were relieved and anxious to see them. They were happy to see us plus the food and fresh water we'd brought. Of course, we asked many questions and they told us how things were going. We also were told an *apparently watered-down version* telling about the brief squabble between Mark and Peter. It was an open and honest discussion between all of us and we told the boys quite plainly that if they were tired and wished to discontinue the venture down the river, no one was forcing them to complete the journey. The four boys were aghast that we should even suggest the termination of their trip. The subject was dropped."

The Meeting according to the kids:
"Our parents informed us that a radio station in Kerrville, KERV, had gotten wind of our trip and that they wanted as many reports on our progress as possible and that they were planning to broadcast an update every time we had anything to report!

"All of a sudden, our trip took on new meaning. If we had ever entertained thoughts of not continuing with our journey, the very idea of quitting now was pushed to the back of our minds. We found it interesting that anyone might find this canoe trip worthy of a radio broadcast!

"After our parents left that Sunday afternoon, we looked at each other in a new way and even though cynical jokes flew all around, inside we felt proud and a little bit embarrassed. Nevertheless, we are ready to go on and look forward to tomorrow's surprises."

Day Eight, June 14, Monday

Peter's Journal and memories

"We got up early and traveled hard for 13 hours. Water became beautiful and the bottom of the river was all gravel. The bottom could be seen down to four feet. Wildlife has become abundant in this area.

Very large mussel found near Seguin

"Somewhere around the boundary line between Guadalupe and Gonzales Counties, we came upon a stretch of water where an underground pipeline had apparently been laid across the river. The bottom was clean gravel and the water, was 8 or 9 feet deep, and was almost as clear as a swimming pool. Alligator gar almost as long as our canoes were resting on the surface. James tried to kill one with his machete only to have his blow glance off the hard head of the fish without any serious damage. The gar merely submerged and swam lazily away.

"The water was so inviting we decided to stop for a refreshing swim, and I discovered by standing on the bottom very cold water coming up through the gravel. I don't know whether the pipeline disturbed the water table or there had always been springs flowing up through the bed of the river, but it was definitely spring water judging from the temperature.

"This was also the day of our first snake-fighting experience. A diamondback water snake had a perch halfway in his mouth and was having difficulty swallowing it the rest of the way. A cottonmouth was lying opposite the diamondback as if it was waiting the outcome to see if it could steal the perch.

"When we approached, the cottonmouth slithered into the water and crossed to the bank on the other side where it stopped. Mark grabbed my long machete and jumped into the bow of one canoe and was paddled across to the cottonmouth. As he drew near the cottonmouth coiled and struck, and Mark blindly—*I swear his eyes were closed*—swung the machete, cutting the head clean off the moccasin."

James and Mark with the headless cottonmouth moccasin and the diamond back

Don's Journal on the same Monday's events:

"Today we broke camp early, were in our canoes and back on the river by 7:15 A.M. We had eggs and bacon for a change. They sure tasted good.

"We took our first break of the day around 11:00 A.M. and ate some chocolate chip cookies. We were all either tired or bored or *something was wrong with our camaraderie.* But, we went on. At 1:15 we ate fried chicken—15 pieces between us— and Mark was still hungry! He's the smallest one of us in size!

"We took about an hour for lunch then rowed on until about 4:00 P.M. and took another break. I still felt down in spirits but Peter started talking to me and that seemed to pick me up. The river seemed a whole lot better and we ran about 9 out of 10 rapids. About 5:30 the water was so clear that we swam till 6:00.

"We continued paddling down the river then until we came to a man checking a trotline—it was 6:45. He said that the bridge on Hwy 80 was about 1 and ½ miles further down the river. We felt good about that. Unfortunately it was more like 4 miles down river and we got to (Taylor's Fishing Camp) about 8:30 P.M. That meant we'd been on the river about 13 and ½ hours today. We were tired and we couldn't have gone on much further.

"I finally got to sleep in the hammock I'd brought. It's lightening and thundering pretty bad tonight.

"After today we are mighty hunters on the Guadalupe. Mark killed one cotton mouthed moccasin."

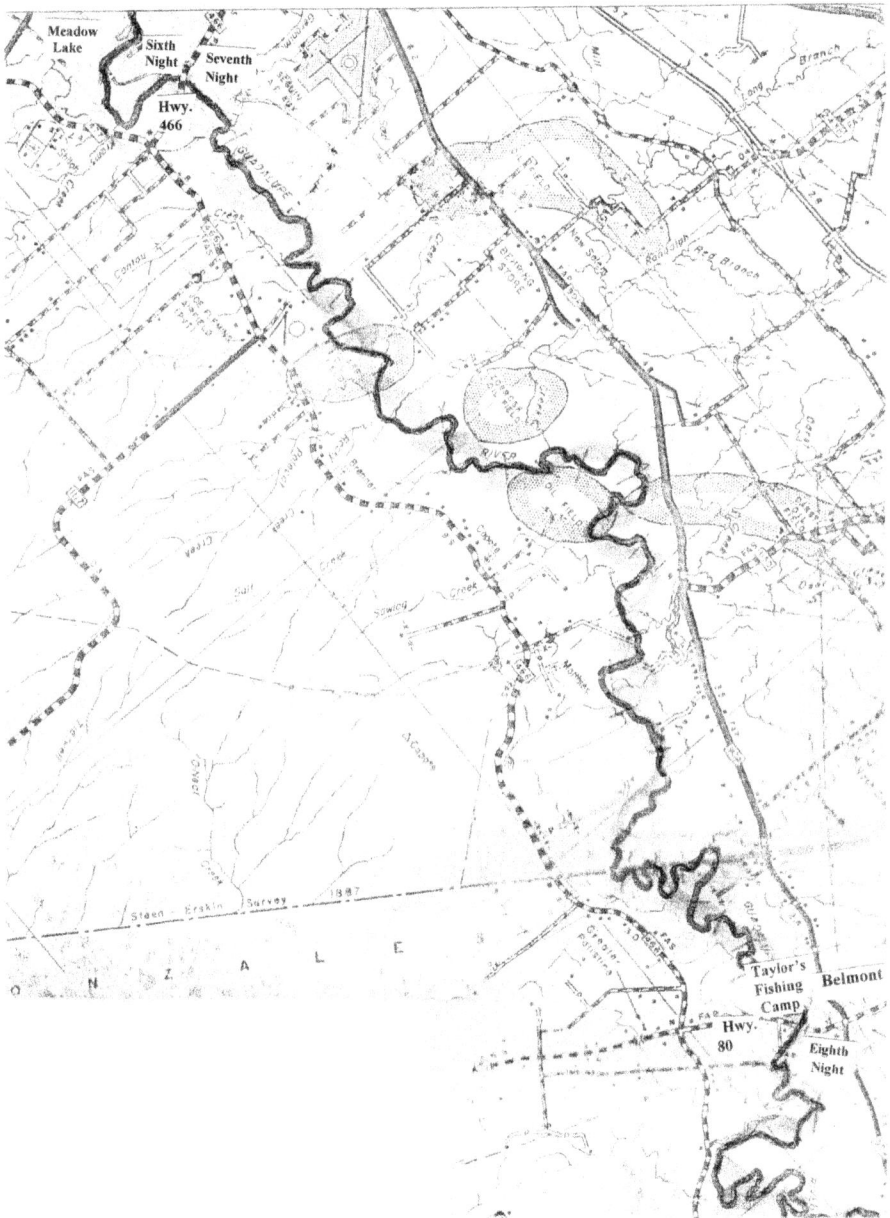

Map of Day Eight

16

Day Nine, June 15, Tuesday

Peter Krauter's Journal:

"We all slept under picnic table verandas since it rained during the night. We left late after deciding that the rain would let up soon. It let up, however, only to make the day hot and humid. Water around Lake Gonzales and below is very dirty and trashy. This evening a wind has begun to blow and there are rain clouds. There's thundering overhead. That's all we need.

"On this day we discovered an old hydroelectric plant. We stopped and crawled all over to explore. Don decided to take a swim in the pool created here. I found a window up high to take pictures and took one of Don swimming below. I continued searching for another window that I could lean out to take a photo looking straight down to the water. I saw the concrete foundation below which was barely above the surface of the water. There were a dozen or more large, cottonmouth moccasins warming themselves in the morning sun.

"We spent the night in this hydroelectric plant—with the landowners permission."

From Don's journal (Same Tuesday)

"We got a late start because of rain. We didn't start rowing until 10:00 A.M. The water wasn't too good so I figured that we didn't make over 18 or 19 miles—maybe only 16. We stopped at 6:30 because of tiredness and so many flies and ticks."

We crawled all over this old hydroelectric plant.

Above: *Clipper and Cleaner*
Left: *Old portable cotton gin?*

Hydroelectric control panel

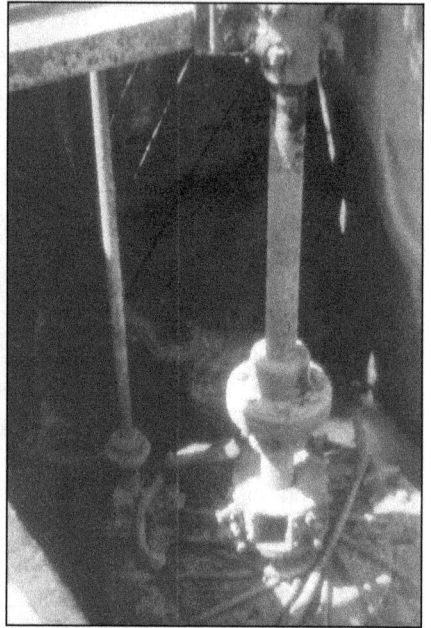

Generator turbine

There were a dozen or more large cotton-mouth moccasins warming themselves in the morning sun

The tiny speck in the second window frame is Don swimming below

Map of Day Nine

17

Day Ten, June 16, Wednesday

Journal by Don:
  "We left at our usual 7:20 this morning ..."

Peter's journal telling of the morning ...
  "Not far down river from the hydroelectric plant where we had spent the night with the landowner's permission, we met a flat-bottom Jonboat making its way up river under the power of a small outboard motor. In the bow sat a large man, maybe in his late twenties to early thirties, wearing overalls and a white t-shirt.

  "In the stern, handling the outboard, was a small, wiry man, possibly in his fifties but definitely marked by greater age and exposure to life, wearing a denim shirt and jeans with a straw hat. The large man in the bow was holding a mayonnaise jar half-filled with a clear liquid, which I immediately assumed was probably *moonshine*, but I was too polite as to inquire regarding its composition.

  "As we approached each other, the pilot of the jonboat shut down the motor and we exchanged greetings. The younger man of great volume asked us where we were headed. We answered, 'To the coast.' After a hearty laugh at our response, the man asked where we had started from, and we answered 'up near Kerrville' knowing that most people back then didn't know the small town of Comfort existed.

"Upon hearing this, all laughter stopped and a look of amazement swept across the younger man's face while the older man shook his head in apparent disbelief that anyone would make such a journey. After exchanging a few more pleasantries, the two men wished us well and we parted ways."

James Durden's version of this story:

"Okay. Let me preface this story by saying if the movie *Deliverance* had already come out, and if I had seen it before our trip, this experience would have ended the journey—at least for me!

"On this particular morning, we woke up to a low hanging fog that made visibility bad. We had our usual breakfast of powdered eggs, toast, cleaned up the campsite, and loaded up the canoes to shove off down river.

"We proceeded timidly that day since the early morning sun could not penetrate the fog and the river was dangerously littered with lots of boulders and dead falls. The last thing we wanted to do was to the end the trip by wrecking our canoes on an unseen obstruction.

"As we crept down river, we soon became aware of the sound of a motor boat coming *up river*. It obviously wasn't a big boat—sounded more like a small outboard motor struggling against the mild current of the river.

"We strained to get a visual fix on the sound but could not locate it. As the sound grew louder and louder we finally decided that the best way to avoid the boat would be to pull over to the shore and let them pass. The river at this point was not very wide—maybe less then 50 feet. If they had to weave in and out of the rocks and deadfalls like we were—there was no place that could be considered safe other then the shore.

"As we waited, the sound grew louder and louder and it was not until the boat was practically on top of us that we saw them.

The sound was coming from a small jonboat with an outboard motor. The boat was carrying two men—an older man in the middle seat and a younger man in the back at the motor's tiller. Both men, wearing bib overalls, sat with their legs crossed facing forward. The old man in the middle seat had his arms folded across his chest and had a gray beard and a weathered course face. Both were wearing baseball caps.

"Neither man looked to left or right nor seemed to care that the river was fraught with debris that could tear the motor right off their boat. They just stared straight ahead and plowed up the river like an old farmer would plow a field. Apparently, they had made this trip before.

"In front of the old man in the middle seat were two old metal milk cans like dairies use to deliver their milk to the creameries. Obviously, the cans were full since the johnboat was sitting low in the water and turning a wake that left the water lapping mightily at the banks.

"As they passed us, I remember thinking instantly: *moonshiners*! Obviously so did Don, 'cause nobody said a word. We just hoped and prayed that they would pass without noticing us and let us be on our way peaceful like.

"To our relief, if they noticed us, they never indicated as such. As soon as the sound was sufficiently beyond us, we quickly pulled back into the main channel of the river and took off. I remember thinking that all I want is to put distance between them and us! That's just what we did!"

Returning to Don's journal:
"We really hauled it to Gonzales. We walked to town there and ate chicken fried steak and club steak and by the time we got back to our canoes it was 3:45 P.M. We ran into some good water and we made it to another pumping station. We had to kill another four-foot cottonmouth for sure and wounded another. We decided to let the others go because we broke one paddle and now only one paddle is left. Mine is cracked—hope it will make it till Sunday."

Same Day—In the Afternoon—and the Snake Encounter That Could Have Ended the Journey!

(Authors note: The following versions of this story are written as the information was given. They are different, yet the same. We will say no more.)

Don's version:

"I guess we thought we were pretty handy with a machete after killing the first cottonmouth. We took a few pictures and re-lived the event, and bragged about how there was no snake safe on the Guadalupe as long as we were around.

"On this Wednesday afternoon, the river had slowed. The maps indicated that the road crossings were few and far between, and we estimated that one stretch was fourteen miles long. There were still some good rapids, but they were getting farther and farther apart, and, in the long still pools in between, boredom again overtook us.

As we paddled, we scanned the banks taking in the natural beauty, looking for things unique.

"As we paddled, our eyes scanned the banks taking in the natural beauty, looking for things unique, and evidence of where we might be. Therefore, it happened that Mark spied a large pile of snake coiled up at the edge of the water next to a dead tree trunk that lay parallel with and a few inches from the water's edge. He called out, 'Hey guys, look over there! Let's get him!'

"We suspended our downstream progress and convened side by side in the middle of the river to develop a plan of attack. With our canoes pointed upstream, paddling intermittently to maintain our location in the slow current, we analyzed the situation. This snake was certainly a lot bigger than the ones we had killed before, so it didn't seem prudent to just walk up and kill it with a 30" long machete. The log protected this pile of snake, so hitting it with a paddle wasn't feasible as long as the snake stayed put.

"Then, someone came up with the idea of lashing a machete to the handle of a spare paddle and stabbing the snake. No one else had a better idea, so James, who was in the bow of the canoe, began to lash his machete to the handle of a paddle using the lining rope.

"Mark and Peter beached their canoe about fifteen yards downstream and positioned themselves a few yards behind each end of the ten foot long log, armed with paddles. If the snake attempted to escape by slithering around one end of the log or the other, one of them would hit the snake with a paddle and stun it long enough to allow a machete stroke.

"While James finished his paddle spear, I let us drift downstream a ways so I could practice my approach. I decided a slow, quiet approach from the downstream side would allow maximum maneuverability of and control over the canoe. This put the snake to our left, allowing James to stab the snake by thrusting the paddle spear with his right hand toward his left side. He practiced a few jabs at make believe targets on the bank, and declared we might as well give it a go.

"Everything was set. Mark and Peter were stationed near the ends of the log, ready to club the snake with their paddles. I paddled the canoe quietly upstream about six feet from water's edge. James had his regular paddle handy in case he needed to paddle on short notice. He had his right hand positioned on the blade of the paddle spear, and his left hand where the paddle handle transitioned to the paddle blade. He was cocked and ready to fire. Slowly we approached—fifteen feet, ten feet, no one said a word for fear of startling the reptile—five feet ...

"I was just thinking how huge that pile of snake was when James suddenly thrust the paddle spear into the pile of snake and then all hell broke loose. His aim had been pretty good but he hit the snake—about two feet from the end of its tail! The snake struck back, like a compressed spring. With its cotton-white mouth wide open, the snake struck at the paddle handle where James's left hand had just been, revealing fangs that squirted smelly venom.

"Seeing the fangs squirting venom only three feet way was too much for me and I began to back paddle as fast and hard as I could. If it was too much for me, I can only imagine how James, who was even closer than I was, must have felt. I quickly realized that James had abandoned his paddle spear and was now paddling forward as hard and fast as he could with the re-sult being that we were going absolutely nowhere!

"I can only guess that all the yelling and paddling was too much for the cottonmouth, too. When James dropped the pad-dle spear, it dislodged itself from the snake's tail. Confronted with the suddenly churning water and commotion in front of it, the snake opted to retreat back toward the log. What we did not know was that the pile of snake had concealed an opening under the log, and the snake headed through that opening, right between Peter and Mark, both of whom were expecting it to come around the one end of the log or the other.

"James and I were yelling that it was getting away and trying to explain that it was not going around the log, but under it. Mark saw the snake's head emerge from under the log, and fig-ured out what was happening. He adjusted his footing and tried to hit the snake with his paddle as it came out from under the log. Unfortunately, his aim was a little off and the paddle struck the log and broke off part of the blade.

"I guess that poor snake was probably wondering what he had done wrong, since every direction he turned someone seemed to be out to get him. He quickly reversed his course and started to enter the water, only to be confronted with James and I—still yelling and still paddling like crazy—and, unfortunately still in opposite directions.

"The snake again reversed its course and decided to make

another try at escape though the hole under the log. This time Mark was ready and swung his paddle. Whether he hit the snake of not, I truly do not know. What I do know is that what was left of his paddle *broke again*, and the snake withdrew from the escape hole under the log and crawled upstream along the log, more or less as we originally anticipated it might. As it passed the end of the log, Mark gave it another whack. It crawled about ten more feet and Mark walked over and finished it off with a few more blows to the head. Mark was a good drummer in the high school band and he thumped that snake's head like a snare drum.

"When James and I finally stopped paddling, I realized that the piece of paddle in Mark's hand was only about eighteen inches long! We poked around on the snake and made sure it was dead. Then, using sticks, we examined its fangs and took pictures, and celebrated another victorious encounter with the snakes of the Guadalupe.

"However, not much later, as we resumed our progress to the coast, our excited conversation gradually faded away into silence. In that hush, I think all of us began to more fully understand the relationship between bravery and *stupidity*, and to realize that what we had just done was *incredibly stupid*.

"Someone finally broke the silence with the questions that were on all of our minds. *What would we have done if one of us had been bitten? It was a good half day to the next crossing and once we got there, we had no idea how far down that road it would be to help. Our progress would be slowed because the victim would not be able to paddle and would have to ride in a canoe with two others, increasing the draft and slowing down the canoe. Would we have attempted a cross-country trek to locate a farm house? Other than attempting to suck the venom from the injection site, and apply a tourniquet, what could we have done? How long could you survive after being bitten?*

"There weren't any good answers. We agreed that from now on, we would not go out of our way to pick any more fights with snakes on this trip."

James Durden's version:

"… the subject of our snake battle? What can I say? I'm older and wiser now and know what a foolish thing we did. At the time, it seemed like a normal part of the canoe trip.

"At first, or maybe I should say, in our first encounter, the snakes didn't stand a chance. Like the the other day when we spotted the two snakes on the bank right at the water's edge. One was a cottonmouth and the other, I thought, a rattlesnake. The cottonmouth had caught a good-sized perch and was in the process of trying to dislocate its lower jar so it could swallow the fish whole while the rattlesnake appeared to be attempting to dislodge the fish from the cottonmouth's mouth and was therefore pretty intent on ignoring us in favor of pursuing its next meal. As we approached with our machetes, neither snake made any effort whatsoever to try to get away and they were dispatched with a single blow—each whack strategically placed immediately behind their triangular shaped heads. We took pictures, patted ourselves on the back and thought we had found yet another ingenious way to rid the Guadalupe of yet another nuisance. Little did we know that this melancholy encounter would lead to an almost trip-ending episode!

"Now I've never been a big fan of snakes. In fact, I would just as soon turn around and go the other way when encountering any snake in the wild. I admit it! I don't even like pictures of snakes in a book or magazine. They make me nervous and send a cold chill down my spine. For as long as I can remember it has always been this way. But, for some reason I don't understand, killing those two snakes earlier made me believe that I had somehow managed to miraculously overcome my natural dislike for the creatures.

"So, spotting a mature cottonmouth laying on the bank, I directed Don to it and told him to ready for the attack. I taped my machete to the end of a spare paddle. Why not—no need to get any closer then necessary. As Don paddled me in towards our foe, I lowered the machete/spear into position. Just as we got close enough to thrust the machete into the seemingly sleeping moccasin it lunged—striking at the machete with mouth open wide, fangs extended, and venom pouring from its fangs. The nauseating stench of venom immediately permeated the air as the snake's lunge struck the machete knocking it and the paddle from my grasp. I quickly tried to melt away into the midsection of the canoe—yelling and screaming for Don to backup! The snake recoiled for what I was sure was going to be another strike, or *possibly a leap into the canoe with us*, I grabbed my normal paddle and began feverishly trying to back paddle clear of the ever increasingly dangerous situation.

"Naturally, as usually happens when things go so unexpectedly wrong, Don and I had a serious communications problem which left us producing more of a churning. We were going nowhere fast!

"Meanwhile, our circumstances, our noise, and the attempt to beat a hasty retreat apparently was enough to confuse the snake into thinking that perhaps he had struck out at something out of his league. He decided to retreat to the other side of the log instead of striking a second time.

"By now, Peter and Mark were also in on the attack and had approached from that side of the log. The snake got to the other side just in time to sustain a blow from Mark's spare paddle, which promptly broke in two. Then Mark, with seemingly fearless abandon, jumped out of the canoe and began pounding the snake's head with the remaining half of his paddle! As Mark delivered repeated blows to the snake his paddle handle continued to break from half a paddle to a quarter of a paddle to an eighth of a paddle until all he had left was a short stick no more then a foot in length. Mark finally quit beating—probably from exhaustion—and deemed the snake dead—much to our relief.

"This incident made us all take a step back and reconsider what had just happened and to contemplate how things might have turned out much, much worse. If the snake had managed to strike any one of us or, if something as simple as getting venom in an open wound, eye or mouth had occurred—our trip would have been over, or possibly even worse, one or more of us *could have died*. We all agreed the foolish risk just didn't seem to be in keeping with the spirit or the adventure of our trip. We made a pact: Unless attacked, *our snake killing is curtailed*.

"We often talk about guardian angels that watch over us and protect us from bad things. I honestly believe we had such help on our trip down the river. The snake incident is proof positive as far as I am concerned."

We often talked about guardian angels that watched over us and protected us from bad things. I honestly believe we had such help on our trip down the river. The snake incident is proof positive as far as I am concerned.—James Durden

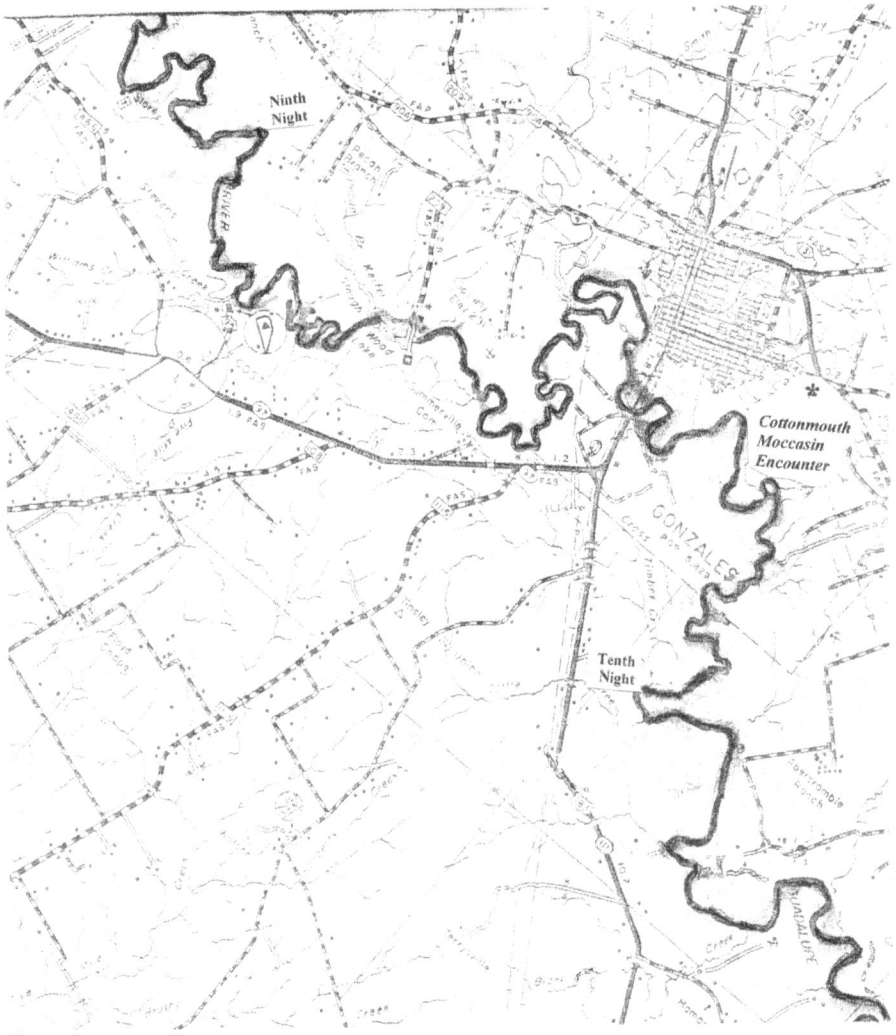

Map of Day Ten

18

Day Eleven, June 17, Thursday

From Don's journal:

"We started out early again and made pretty good time. The water was really nice with lots of good rapids. We're at Hochheim now and resting. The sun is going down and we're still reliving our snake encounter for about the sixth time. It's still a chilling story.

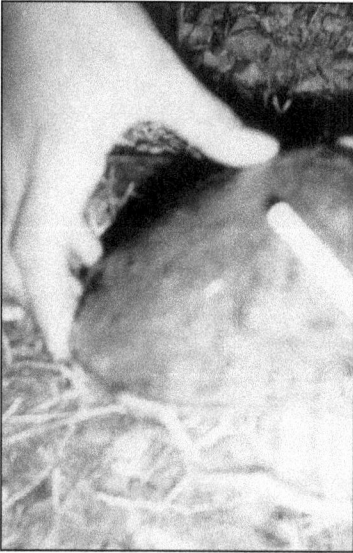
Large turtle we caught today

"We have studied our maps and we think we can make it to our two crossings and our planned a meeting place with our parents again by Sunday.

"It has been a long day and it was nearly dark when we finally reached an old style fishing camp, with concrete tables and benches, each covered by a tin roof supported by steel pipes. Finally, the distance and stability of the pipes were perfect for our hammocks!

"There were little barbeque pits and we used them to cook

our evening meal of freeze dried eggs and hot chocolate. We were grateful for their potable water supply and filled all of our water jugs and canteens. As we settled into our bed rolls (army blankets), we could see lightning in the distance.

Map of Day Eleven

19

Day Twelve, June 18, Friday

Don's Journal:

"This morning we awoke to light, intermittent drizzle. We briefly considered waiting to see what the weather would do, but soon decided that we might as well get started. The clouds would at least help block the hot sunshine.

"We left our campsite at 7:15 after a breakfast of sweet rolls, cokes, jelly beans, peanut brittle, cookies and Fritos. The water was the best we've run into yet and we made really fine time.

"The morning passed quickly and it looked like the weather was going to clear. Following a tuna sandwich and a few chips for lunch, we paddled for an hour and broke for about 15 minutes. For the last two or three days we've been following a practice of paddling for an hour and then resting for 10-15 minutes. Surprisingly, we make really good time that way.

"The afternoon heating cooked up some thunderstorms and soon one of them was upon us. At first, it wasn't too bad. The rain was cool and refreshing. Then suddenly, the wind came up and the rain was feeling cold. Lightning flashed and thunder clapped as the rain came down so hard we had to bail water out of the canoes. James was having a hard time seeing with rain on his glasses, and we were all second guessing our decision to leave the sanctuary of Taylor's fish camp. Mostly because we didn't see that we had any other good options, we pressed on for another hour or so more in the incessant rain, hoping to find some sort of shelter to which to retreat.

"The rain kept up and got worse. Then the wind came up harder and we were freezing. After an hour and a half we decided to stop at the first house or bridge we'd find. We found neither.

"Thirty minutes later we caught a wind from the back and from the side at the same time ... like it was

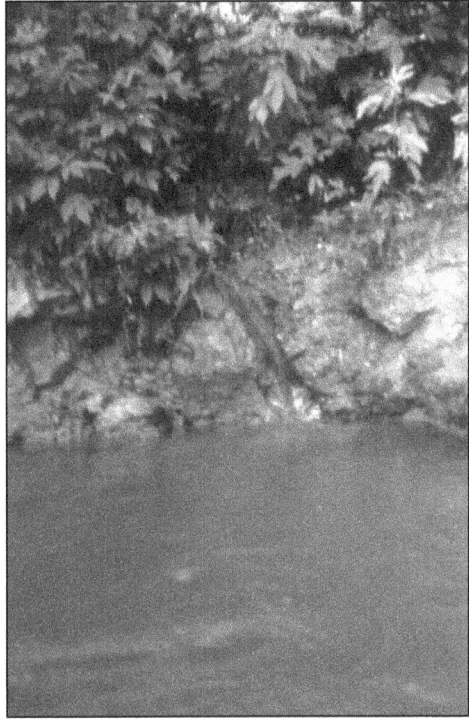

A strong spring gushes out of the bank.

swirling. Growing up we all had spent a lot of time outdoors and were not necessarily frightened by severe weather, but we all knew we should respect it. With all the heavy thunder and lightning, I was wondering if we were in or on the fringe of a tornado or twister when suddenly there was an exceptionally bright flash of lightning accompanied by an almost immediate boom of thunder. We all looked around to see a large dead tree on the left bank and saw what looked like a smoking buzzard hanging in its upper limbs. After a brief consultation, we decided the prudent thing to do would be to *get off the water quick* and we pulled out on a gravel bar.

"We were exceptionally cold and wet by now and Peter and Mark decided to seek refuge under their canoe. James and I decided to see if we could find a barn or goat shed and took off on foot going cross-country. It was still raining, but not quite as hard and we soon came to a small ravine running bank full with rain water about twenty feet wide. Not wanting to abandon the path we were on, we decided to wade across and continue on our way.

"I waded in the swift water slowly at first, testing each foot hold. The ground seemed steep as I progressed and soon I was almost waist deep and not even half way across. Suddenly, it felt as though the ground moved out from under me. Either I stepped into a gulley or the wall of the gulley gave way. Regardless, I found myself fully submerged in the rushing water without a foothold.

"If you've never found yourself swimming in floodwater, you don't have an appreciation for the debris that is in there with you—leaves and branches, rocks and dirt, cow manure and

We wondered, with all the rain and heavy thunder and lightening, if we were on the fringe of a tornado. Suddenly there was an exceptionally bright flash of lightening accompanied by an almost immediate boom of thunder. We all looked around, saw a large dead tree on the left bank, and saw a smoking buzzard hanging in the upper limbs. We knew we needed to get off the river fast!

fencing wire, and whatever else the water gobbles up on its way downstream. The current, which on the surface appears mostly to run in one direction (downstream), actually moves up and down, and back and forth, making swimming feel more like climbing a waterfall.

"Once I got my head back up and got a breath of air, I was able to gradually negotiate my way across the gulley, get my feet under me, and get out on the other side. Somehow, James had managed to get across more gracefully than I had and we resumed our muddy march.

"Within a few minutes, we came upon a gravel road. We talked briefly about which direction to go, and then turned right, and began to follow it. We had taken only a few steps when a pickup crested the hill in front of us and headed our direction. I guess we must have looked pretty desperate. The driver, an old cowboy, stopped, and in a tone that didn't reveal either contempt or concern, asked where we were going. We told him we were going to the coast on the Guadalupe, and had been forced off the river by the thunderstorm, and asked if he knew of someone who might have a shed or barn nearby that we could get in to dry out for the night. Without answering the question, he asked where we started and how long we had been on the river. In retrospect, I am sure he must have been checking us out to make sure our somewhat incredulous tale was legitimate. (How many people have you encountered walking down a gravel road who claimed to be on the way to the coast? And if you did, would you believe their story?)

"What we didn't know at the time, but learned later, was that news of our adventure had made the Cuero newspaper. Coming upon us in the state we were in, he put two and two together and figured we must have been half of the party. Our corroboration of the account in the newspaper was good enough to win him over and he warmed up to us considerably.

"He advised us that he owned the land we had just crossed and that we were welcome to spend the night in an old farm house nearby. That sounded mighty good to us and we did not

Youths Tackling River in Canoes

Four youths from Comfort in Kendall County, on the far upper reaches of the Guadalupe River, hope to pass Cuero this weekend on a canoe journey to the Coast.

Paddling two canoes loaded with supplies, water and river maps, they left Comfort at 8 a.m. on Monday, June 7. They rested Sunday in Seguin, where they were met by parents bringing supplies and enjoyed a picnic with their families.

Making the trip in the summer heat are Donald Durden, 17, and James Durden, 15, sons of Mr. and Mrs. Jerry Durden Jr.; Peter Kreuter, 15, son of Mr. and Mrs. James Kreuter; and Mark Rausch, 16, son of Mr. and Mrs. Hubert Rausch, all of Comfort.

Parents reported the boys one day ahead of schedule at their Seguin stop.

The youths said their saddest experience until then had been encountering "extreme pollution" at some places in the river.

In those places the stench was "enough to make you sick," they said.

Happiest experience has been the helpful people they met along the way, who gave them much aid in the way of advice and instruction.

Crossing Canyon Lake was the most exciting part of the trip, they said. Contrary to some reports, they made it across on their own.

"Man, we paddled it—we were not towed."

The youths have averaged 20-22 miles a day, with their best mileage being the stretch from New Braunfels to Seguin in one day.

"We won't try that again," the boys told Mr. Durden Sunday.

"We were so tired we were ready to drop and morale was at a low, low point. Speed is not our objective anyway."

hesitate a second in accepting his offer. He gave us directions to the house, told us to make ourselves at home and to leave the place like we found it. We asked him to please call our parents to let them know we were safe. He agreed and we gave him the telephone number in Comfort."

"There were two small hitches: We had to go back about 1 and ½ miles to get Mark and Peter and then carry our food and ammo boxes and dry clothes 2 miles to the house all in the still driving rain. But we did it and made it okay.

"James and I headed back to get Mark and Peter. As we approached, with our own personal tidings of great joy, Mark and Peter emerged from under their canoe, covered with sand, dirt, leaves, and cow manure. After teasing them about their *crappy appearance*, we secured the canoes, gathered up what we needed for the night and headed out to the farmhouse.

We were so thankful for the kindness and generosity of a softhearted old cowboy and the prevenient Grace of God who put us in his path.—Don

"That night we had a great time. We took showers—hot showers and changed into dry clothes. We warmed up a big can of beef stew and some canned vegetables we had been saving for a special occasion, and enjoyed dinner at a real table with real chairs and slept in real beds. We slept well that night thankful for the kindness and generosity of a softhearted old cowboy, and the prevenient Grace of God who put us in his path."

Meanwhile, the Peter Krauter and Mark Rausch Story

"We started out after a good night's sleep at the bridge at Hochheim. Everyone felt strong so we made real good time in the morning even though the sun was radiating brightly.

"After dinner, we rested awhile, then continued under threatening thunderheads. Around 2:00 P.M., rain began to pour, not drizzle. I jumped in the river and everyone followed since it was warm in the water. Finally, we got back in the canoes and continued on to try and make it to the Highway 766 crossing.

"The heavy rain was constant and threatening with high water. We fought to keep going, until wind became too wild and the river started getting higher. We finally pulled the canoes on to high ground.

"Don and James went to find some place for us to stay, while Mark

Mustang grape vines

and I unloaded the canoes, turned them over, and crowded under them in the mud and cow manure!

"In an hour, Don and James came back with the good news that we were going to stay in a hunting cabin tonight, because an old man had read about us in the Cuero newspaper and had a big heart!

"So, here I am—resting on a big bed of my own. There are about 14 beds in here! Don cooked beef stew and coffee on the electric stove and we had a fancy supper on good china with nice silverware. We all took showers and baths. This place has everything! Once again, we're looking forward to talking to our parents day after tomorrow. By the way, last we heard, the rainfall was *6 inches*!

"We played poker for a while that night. I still have the Pan American Airlines deck of cards we used that night. We carried them in an empty Marlboro cigarette pack.

James Durden remembers this night also.

"Close to Cuero we encountered a fairly severe thundershower that managed to run us right off the river. We were pretty intent on pressing on through the rain, but it quickly became obvious that we were spending more time bailing than we were paddling. We weren't really getting anywhere.

"While we'd gotten pretty used to being wet—getting soaked to the bone was something we were not prepared for. We had no slickers or raincoats or even a tent. It didn't take long before the rain made everyone extremely uncomfortable. There was also a lot of lightning overhead and thunder was cracking off the banks of the river adding an eerie sensation of bad things to come.

"As we rounded a bend in the river, almost as if something told all of us simultaneously to look down the river and there, high in the top of a dead but still standing cypress tree was a buzzard lodged in the forks of the tree's upper limbs! It was on its back, claws and talons straight up to the sky, and it was smoking and smoldering. Either that buzzard had been struck directly

by lightning or the lightning had struck the tree where it had selected to seek refuge from the storm. Either way, we didn't really
care. We got the message: *We needed to get off the river and out
of the weather and we needed to do it now!*

"We put in on the starboard bank of the river and proceeded
to hold a standing-in-the-rain group meeting about what we
should do for shelter. We all knew about Guadalupe River
floods. They can be sudden and they can be quite severe. We
agreed that we needed at least to get out of the immediate
riverbed.

"Another problem we faced now was the deep gorge carved
by the river through the Texas coastal plain. Where we had
landed there were good gravel bars along the immediate
riverbed but the bank cut up very steeply a good 20 or 30 feet
to the natural ground elevation. Portaging the canoes and all our
cargo up those muddy banks would be impractical if not impossible—at least until we had a better feel for how the river was
going to react to the storm.

"After discussing several options, we decided that Mark and
Peter would stay with the canoes. They would secure what they
could to keep things as dry as possible while Don and I would
try to get up the bank and scout around for shelter away from
the river.

"We took off slipping and sliding our way up the muddy
bank until we reached flat ground. We struck out directly away
from river hoping to find a road or some sign of human occupa-
tion.

"We crossed a large grown-over field adjacent to the river
and then we found an unpaved county road. General knowledge of where we were indicated the best direction to go to find
people would be to turn north on the road. That's what we did.

"We had only gone a few steps when we heard that wonder-
fully familiar sound of crunching gravel as a vehicle came traveling down this unpaved country road. Even in the rain that
sound came through loud and clear.

"We spun around to see a pickup pulling up to us. The driver stopped and asked us what in the world we were doing out in such a rainstorm. We explained our situation and that we had two friends back at the river and asked the man if he had a barn or porch or somewhere we could hole-up until the storm passed. The man's friendliness and eagerness to help us plus his real concern for our safety soon had us giving thanks to the Almighty that we had amazingly ended up *exactly where we did!*

"We went back to the river and found Mark and Peter sheltering themselves and all our cargo under overturned canoes. We secured the canoes, grabbed our personal stuff, and *with the man driving the truck*, he took us to the *Guadalupe Hilton*—a hunting cabin with a roof—dry floors—cooking facilities—and even *inside* plumbing!

"The night we spent at that cabin was the most peaceful and restful night I can recall from the entire trip. We actually got to eat a hot meal prepared on a real stove and then ate it at a real dining table! Such wonderful luxury for just a simple hunting cabin! Amazing how fast one can learn to appreciate the simple

We actually paused to give thanks. We got to eat a hot meal prepared on a real stove and then ate it at a real dining table! Such wonderful luxury ... amazing how fast on can learn to appreciate the simple things.—James

things. It is even more amazing how quickly *one forgets how wonderful the simple things are.* If this night had been just another night at home I have no doubt we would have never even given the meal and the circumstance a second thought. After all this time on the river, I was not so sure we had not died and gone to heaven!

"The night we spent in the hunting cabin has another interesting story. Peter and I soon discovered (while looking for bedding) that the lid on a storage trunk had a spring assisted mechanism which, when the lid was raised in the front, caused the lid to jump forward and upward with a hefty degree of force. It was as if something on the inside was pushing up on the lid to jump out at you. For two kids in a strange house under even stranger circumstance this seemed like the perfect gag to setup the older guys for a good laugh.

"So Peter got his camera setup and I went and got Mark with some lame story about coming to look at this trunk—that I wasn't sure—but it seemed like something had bumped inside it and I needed him to take a look.

"Okay, I agree, I did sort of set him up to be overly cautious before he even attempted to open the lid. But he got the same bit of a jolt when the lid jumped and Peter and I got a good laugh anyway. We pulled the same ruse on Don and got the same results.

"I find it interesting that despite traveling through some of the most scenic parts of Texas with a very limited amount of photographic material and limitless photographic opportunities that we managed to capture both Mark and Don cautiously lifting the lid on the spooky trunk. Just goes to show how goofy kids can be!

"The next morning dawned bright and sunny and we knew we had to leave. Don penned a heartfelt thank-you note from all of us and we took up a collection to leave Mr. McCurdy a token of our gratefulness. It wasn't much— just some odd dollars and cents—but we wanted him to know how much we appreciated the hospitality and his kindness."

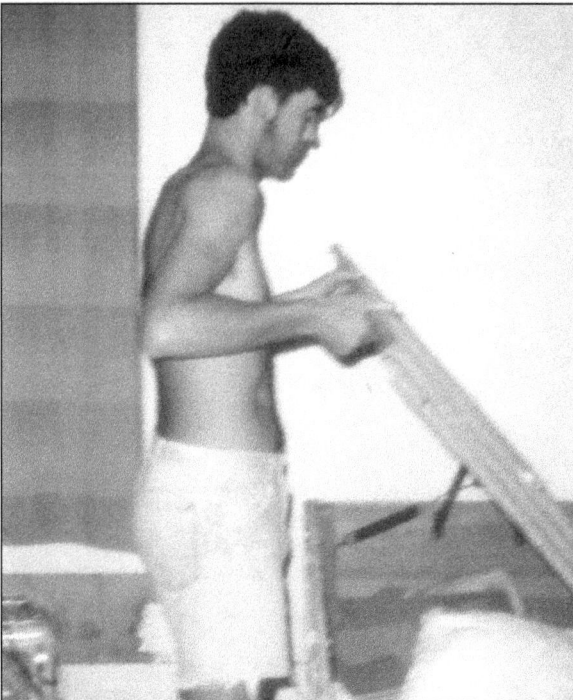

Peter set up his camera and James set up this gag on the older guys.

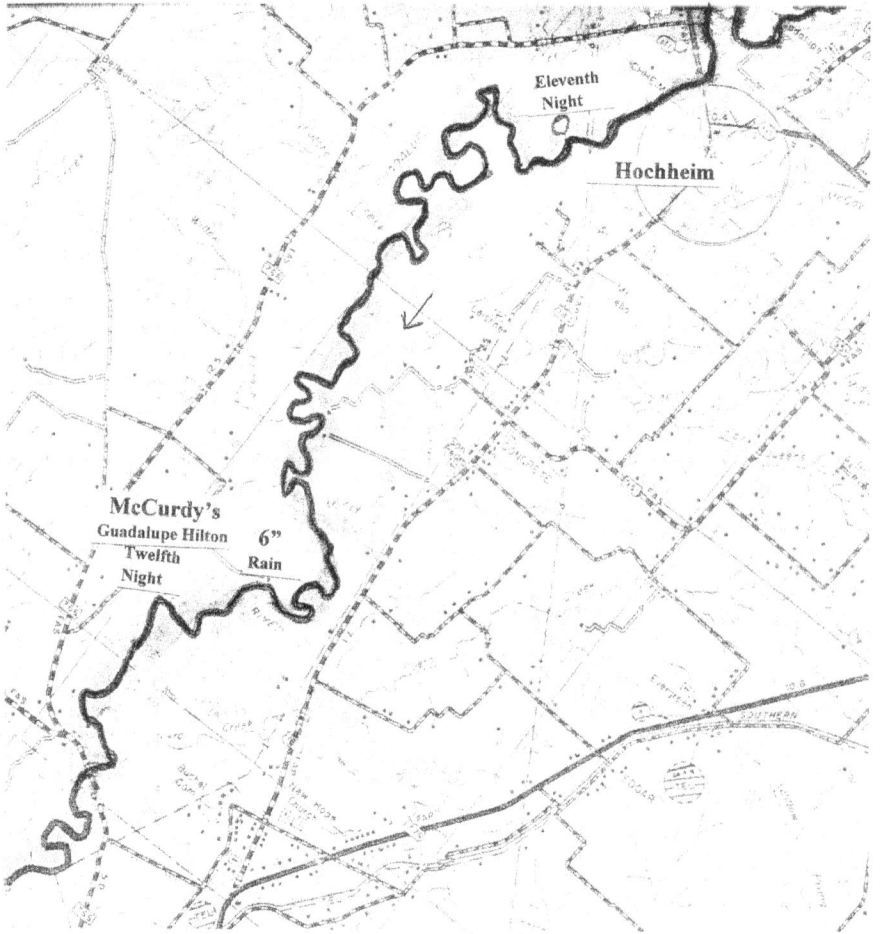

Map of Day Twelve

Day Thirteen, June 19, Saturday

Journal by Don:

"Everybody was really in good spirits this morning. We had good water today, paddling went well, and our goal is in sight. I feel now that the worst part of the trip is over. We expect to have good water here on out. When we started, I had no feeling about the end because I was smitten with the beginning. I had been really tired at the start of this week but now I look forward with eager anticipation to the completion of what I think has been a very maturing experience. We have become accustomed to our river life and while the camp house was nice, the river is not that bad. We're about three days ahead of our schedule now.

"We made it to the bridge at Highway 766 and stopped to put out some orange flagging to let our parents know we'd passed this point. About 100 yards after that it started to rain again. We turned around and went back to take cover under the bridge again and stayed there for about one and a half hours until the rain stopped.

"It was still damp but we paddled on now and reached an abandoned CPL dam. After exploring there for a while the rain began again. Because it did not look like it would stop, we decided to spend the night inside there.

111

"One funny incident happened in the group at this plant. Mark, James, and I shot the bull until 11 P.M. We were still not sleepy. So, Mark and I decided to make the bridge that night by leaving at 12 midnight or 2:00 A.M. When that time came, our beds looked a lot nicer than that hard canoe seat. (We traveled only about 3 miles today.)

For Boys Only—A Classic Vignette

About that night from James...

"We decided to go exploring inside an old abandoned GBRA dam building and discovered that it would make an excellent place to spend the night. It had clean, metal floors and a sound roof. We even built a small fire on the metal floor and settled in for a peaceful night.

"At some point in the evening, somebody *passed gas*. This was not a rare occurrence for *this* crew and most of the time it happened without much more then the typical *guy* comments. Tonight it was different. We were indoors and in close quarters!

"Frankly, it was bad. Really bad. It stunk to high heaven and it garnished a lot more rants, raves and vocal gesticulation than it should have and somewhere along the line Mark Rausch said, "Man! We should have burnt that one!"

"Well, okay, I admit it, being an all male crew, it didn't take long. After many off color comments and challenges Mark said, "Here, I'll show you." He proceeded to lie down on his back, pulled his knees up to his chest, and locked his elbows behind them. He had no more then assumed that position when he struck a match and held the lit thing near his pants in the proximity of his butt. *Faa-voomoom!* Honest! It lit up the whole area with a pale yellow glow!

"Naturally, we were all impressed! That is, all of us except Peter. He seemed to be more intent on getting a good night's sleep then advancing his knowledge of such things. Anyway, just for the record, thanks to that night and Mark's volunteer spirit there will never be any doubt in my mind. You need to *be care-*

ful when approaching a fireplace or wood burning stove.
Sometimes it takes experience to teach us. I will never forget this
incident!

"Yes, Virginia, they do burn! And, quite brightly at that!"

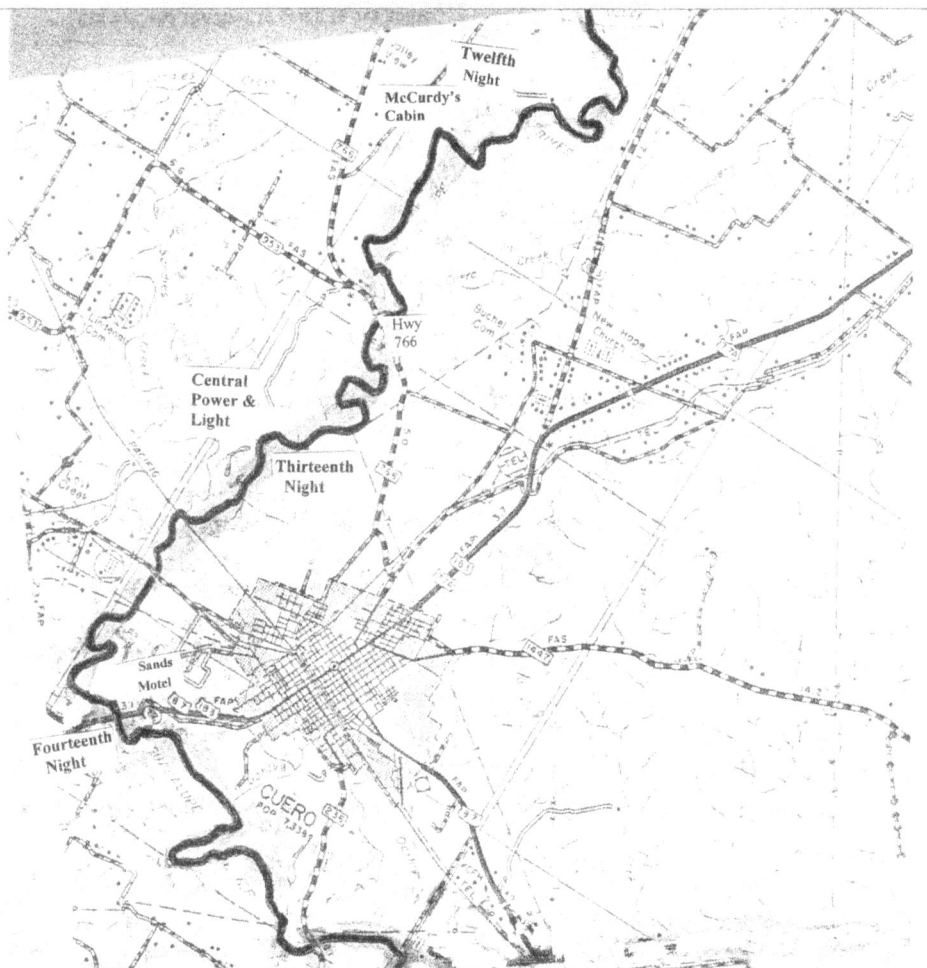

Map of Days 13 and 14

21

Day Fourteen, June 20, Sunday

Don's Journal:

"We paddled from the plant to Cuero where we had arranged to meet our parents. They had a big surprise for us. They had made reservations at the Sands motel in Cuero for our meeting. They said they would stay with us into the late afternoon before they had to go back to Comfort and that we'd get to stay in the motel overnight.

"They had also arranged another nice surprise for us by having Mr. and Mrs. McCurdy—the owners of the Guadalupe Hilton—to meet all of us there at the motel! There was a lot of talk about how the people in Comfort were very concerned about us and the six inch rain on the Guadalupe and how Mr. McCurdy had found us. They said that radio station KERV in Kerrville was still broadcasting news about us.

"Next, they made a really big deal about bringing greetings to the McCurdys from the Comfort Chamber of Commerce. They also presented a big round tea-ring to the McCurdys. Anyway, it was nice to see everybody and all the food stuff they brought for our last week on the river.

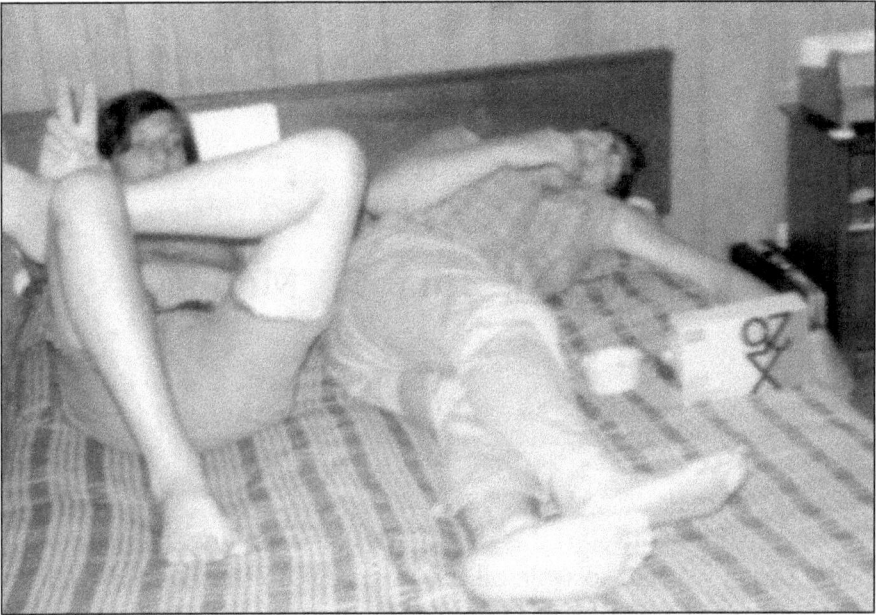

Inside the motel where a meeting with the McCurdys was a surprise for the canoers. Later, Don and Mark just took a nap.

Peter and James relaxing at Sands Motel

22

Day Fifteen, June 21, Monday

Don's Journal:

"We got a late start this morning. After spending the night in the motel we had to walk all the way back to the river! We left around 9:00 A.M. We ate supper at County Bridge and then decided to paddle afterwards—at night—to the Hwy 447 bridge in Victoria County. James fell out of the canoe while running rapids in the dark but he was not hurt. We were lucky and stupid to canoe in the dark ..."

*James also remembers **most vividly***

"What a mess this turned out to be. As I recall we made the decision to travel at night based on two factors. One, we felt we could make better time at night. The other was to avoid the oppressive heat and humidity of the summer days. *Neither proved to be correct.*

"First off, head-worn headlights make very poor illumination to travel by on a river. The light simply reflects off the water and up onto the trees or bank leaving obstacles in the water virtually undetectable. This point was driven home to me when I suddenly spotted a large flat rock approaching immediately to the front right of the canoe.

"The rock looked to be as large as a regular dinner table with a flat top that lurked just inches below the surface of the water. I knew if we continued as we were going we would end up running aground on that rock and possibly capsize. I immediately called out "ROCK! ROCK!" as I stuck my paddle out in an attempt to fend off the stone table and hopefully allow us to pass it by without incurring any harm or damage to the canoe.

"But, because of the poor lighting, I was not able to properly judge the distance to the rock under the water. When my paddle did not strike rock at the anticipated time I quickly found myself not only overextended over the side of the canoe but also blinded as my headlight battery fell overboard pulling my headlight band down over my eyes, knocking my glasses to my chest.

"Almost simultaneously, as I was falling out of the canoe, my paddle struck the top of the rock and was sliding along the surface. It provided a leveraged ramp that guided me directly to the top of the rock! I suddenly found myself sitting in the middle of the river—holding my paddle—groping for my glasses—trying to recover my headlight battery—and trying to relocate my headlight band back to the top of my head so I could see.

"I had no more then pulled off a total *I'm-cool-and-I-know-it* recovery when along came Peter and Mark in their canoe apparently dead set on *running me over!* They said later that when they spotted me in their headlights it looked as if I was sitting on top of the dark water!

"Anyway, I grabbed the bow of their canoe, pushed them clear of the rock. I then began imploring the guys to *please get me the heck off that damn rock!*

"At the very slight cost of a little pride, it was another very good lesson learned. One more time, no one got hurt and no damage was done to either one of the canoes.

"Oh! I should add one good reason not to canoe at night with headlights is the bugs that swarm around a white light on a Texas summer night. We probably spent more time spitting out errant moths from our mouths and chasing bugs out of our ears and nose then we did paddling. Another good reason not to canoe at night is the unknown intimidation of *not having all your senses to rely upon.*

"At one point that night, as we were rounding one of the Guadalupe's infamous bends, we became aware of hearing a growing roar located somewhere just down river. Naturally, we immediately suspected a waterfall or a dam. Not wanting to get caught in either we approached the noise with ever-increasing caution. The louder the noise the slower we went until we were practically doing nothing more then just floating. Imagine our surprise when finally we rounded a bend and discovered a large drainage pipe from an industrial site draining waste water into the river from high up on the bank! Our fears proved unwarranted and we all acknowledged: *River travel is made for the daylight hours—nights are for sleeping!*"

Map of Day Fifteen

Day Sixteen, June 22, Tuesday

Don's Journal:
"We broke camp and were out rowing by 8:00 A.M. Everybody is in good spirits knowing that we are on the tail end of our journey. We made Victoria by 2:00 P.M. We walked to Fossatino's Delicatessen and called our parents and made the spur road our stop for the night.

James Durden: Expounding on another view
"Once we passed all the middle Guadalupe lakes we were very surprised that day around Victoria when we ran headlong into yet another *strange looking* dam across the river. Strange thing was: this dam didn't seem to impound any water; it didn't create a lake or do anything to impede the flow of the river!

"We portaged around the structure for fear of being caught in the suction of its gates. It wasn't until we were alongside the building at the end of the dam that we realized this was a *salt water diversion dam*. Apparently, during times of low flow the old Guadalupe tends to pull salt water out of the Gulf of Mexico and lets it flow inland. This wreaks havoc on farmers who use the natural water resource of the Guadalupe for irrigation. The Department of Agriculture developed this structure to prevent contamination of the fresh river water by salty sea-water. I only remember running into one of these structures during the trip—the other guys seem to remember there being more.

"Another unusual thing that occurred during our portage around the diversion dam was *sighting the upper part of a large ocean-going ship apparently cruising across the coastal plains of Texas!* That's right! We saw a huge

A salt water diversion dam

cargo ship laden with containers and it was steadily heading north across the plains! It wasn't stirring up any dust nor did it seem to be having any difficulty whatsoever with the tough black gumbo soils that make up the geology of this region.

"No! *We hadn't been drinking* nor were we suffering from *group delusion* brought on by too many hours in the South Texas sun. We soon figured it out by consulting our maps. *What we had spotted* was a ship headed up the *Intra-coastal canal that extends up to Victoria!* Because of the slight rolling terrain of the land and the river's near proximity to the canal, our line of vision at one point on the Guadalupe River allowed us to see only the *top of the ship* which was *seemingly passing on the horizon*

while the lower portion of the ship in the canal remained hidden.

"Needless to say—to the four of us in canoes—at the first sighting—the very thought that we might encounter such a ship plowing up the Guadalupe River was a bit un-nerving. We were all very relieved when we finally realized that this encounter was as close as we were going to get to such an occurrence."

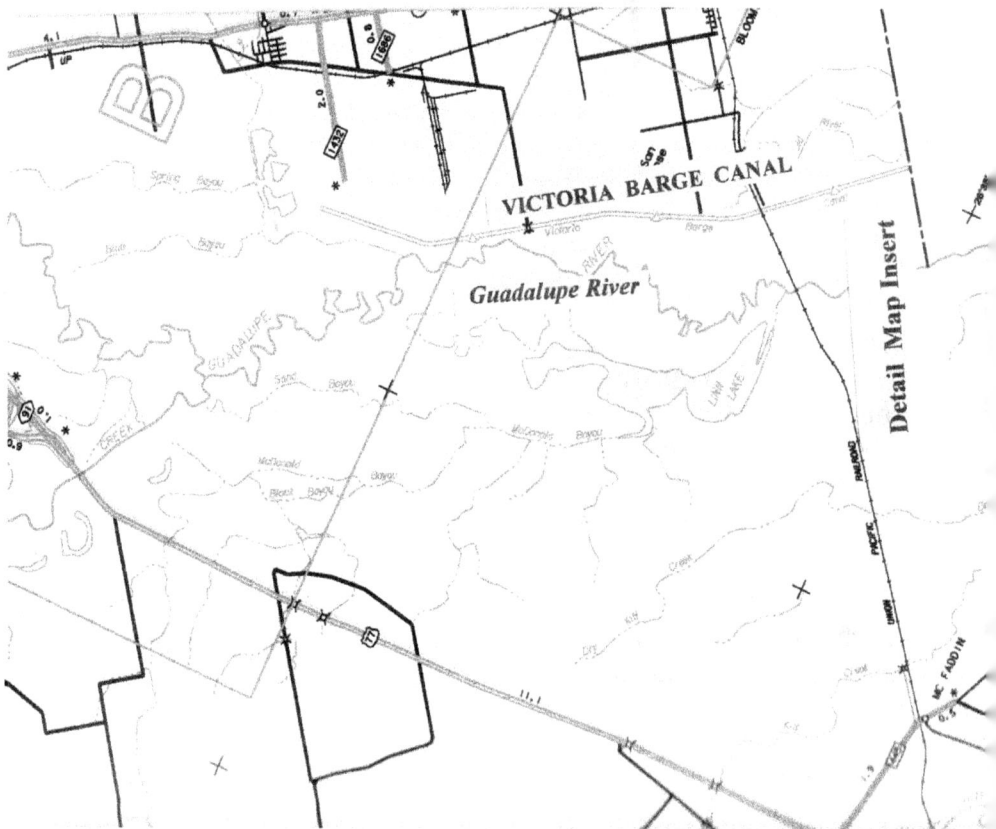

Map shows how the Guadalupe River runs nearby the The Victoria Barge Canal.

Sunset in camp along Guadalupe River

Map of Day Sixteen

Day Seventeen, June 24, Wednesday

Don's Journal
"We started out again at 8:00 A.M. after a breakfast of pancakes fixed by Mark. We couldn't find the egg turner so he used a large enameled spoon. The pancakes turned out lumpy and all balled-up but surprisingly good.

"We made excellent time today and reached the railroad bridge by 5:00 P.M. About 1½ mile more and we faced our first logjam. Never having seen a logjam before, we were surprised to see grass seemingly growing on the water! These log jams proved to be the toughest obstacle of our entire trip.

"Following a scouting trip to decide which route our portage would follow, we began packing our supplies over first. Darkness was quickly coming upon us and we soon found ourselves two miles from camp, loaded with equipment and supplies and being eaten alive by mosquitoes. Upon arrival at camp, we quickly laid out our beds and soaked ourselves with insect repellent. Not a good night."

From Peter Krauter's Journal:
"We didn't really know what a logjam was going to look like, but we were amazed at how the river seemed to just end when

125

Log jam! We were surprised! Grass was seemingly growing on top of where the river was supposed to be!

we reached the beginning of the first jam. Logs and brush were piled up at this point, and silt settled on top of the pile and grass was growing out of the silt. The water apparently flows under and through the logs, but for all appearances the river just seems to stop.

"The portage around the logjam was made much easier due to the landowner having bulldozed a fresh road along the entire length of the jam. The landowner, a doctor who happened to be checking on the roadwork, gave us permission to use this road.

"Even so, we spent

The portage around the log jam was made much easier due to the landowner having bulldozed a fresh road along the entire length of the jam.—Peter

several hours, all four of us, alternately carrying a loaded canoe, one at a time, until we reached the downstream end of the jam—sometime around 10 P.M. We were dead tired and stinking of sweat. We decided to bed down on the fresh earth of the new road since the alternative was covered in deep bunch grasses and brush and *possibly full of snakes.*

"It was hot and humid—even this late at night. I tried to fall asleep on top of my army blankets, but the air was thick with mosquitoes making sleep impossible. Even though I was too hot to sleep, I was also too tired to stay awake and, *ignoring the sounds coming from the nearby brush that I know in my heart were coyotes*, I covered myself with one of my blankets and fell unconscious until morning.

"In the morning we didn't even consider having breakfast even though we'd had no supper the night before. Instead, we packed up and immediately began making our way—carrying the canoes through the brush and weeds—back to the river. I cannot begin to describe how good it felt to once again sit down in the canoe and paddle away from this logjam which had tested our will and perseverance."

James Durden:
"I don't recall when we first heard about the difficulty of log-jams but it seems like it was someone on one of the lakes below New Braunfels who first mentioned them. They told us that as we approached the end of our trip we would need to keep a careful watch out for *logjams* caused by all the debris and tim-ber that was constantly washing down the tree-lined Guadalupe River. We heard stories about how you could be *sucked under* a logjam and drown if you weren't careful. We were also warned that it would not be uncommon to encounter snakes and varmints like alligators and crocodiles around logjams. All in all the wild stories got us to thinking and planning days in advance for our inevitable encounter with the end of the river.

"We therefore had assumed several different scenarios (re-membering what Bob Roberts had told us about *needle and thread* the last stretch of our journey) and we were pretty much ready for the day we came to our first log jam.

"Much of what we had been told was true. The river does disappear from sight. For all appearances, it looked like the river simply stops its journey headlong into a brush-ensnarled embankment. Closer inspection revealed that the embankment was composed of logs, limbs, branches, weeds, random lumber, plastic bottles, Styrofoam, old tires, and just about anything that you have ever seen with the ability to float.

"After centuries and centuries of tirelessly cleaning out its drainage area of these things, the Guadalupe River has managed to create a randomly-generated surface dam far superior to anything man could ever dream up. I suspect it all started simply enough: A log or some other item got pushed into the bank by a small eddy current and got lodged there by repeated coverings with silt and mud. Then, limbs and weeds get caught by that log—more silt and mud buries these items—then perhaps another log comes to rest against the original one—it catches more and more junk—and before you know it the jam stretches all the way across the river.

"Then, year after year of filtering and catching more and more debris, the logjam just grows higher and deeper. All the rich silt and mud covering the jam combines with the fresh water of the river and the jam will soon be covered with lush vegetation of every kind imaginable.

"Thankfully we didn't experience any of the severe under tows or encounter any of the *toothy creatures*. We knew the logjam deserved a healthy dose of respect and so we opted to land our canoes on the starboard bank and scout out the situation.

"Upon landing, we found what appeared to be a freshly opened pasture road which seemed to follow the river's path close enough to make it usable to portage the canoes. The only question was how long was the logjam and how far would we have to carry them?

"As we walked along the road, the heat and humidity was seriously oppressive. The road cut through what can best be described as a brush thicket and there was little to no moving air. What little sunlight got through the thick canopy only managed to create sunbeams that helped make the near 100% humidity almost unbearable. Not only that, but after two weeks on the river in continuous wet conditions the jock rash was running rampant. It was a miserable hike.

"As it turned out, the logjam was over a mile in length. This meant that it would not be possible for each crew to be able to drag or slide their canoe. We would have to carry them—four men to a canoe—two trips would be necessary. This one mile of river easily turned out to be the worst activity of the entire trip."

Map of Day Seventeen

Day Eighteen, June 25, Thursday

Don's Journal:
"We were up by 6:15 and decided to eat no breakfast but instead go directly to the canoes 2 miles away. The two canoes had our equipment in them and consequently were still so heavy that all four of us were required on one canoe if it was to be carried any respectable distance.

"The last 200 yards from camp to the river proved easier than thought and we were in the water by 9:00. We passed the San Antonio River and just around the bend we saw a bridge not shown on our maps. It turned out to be a salt-water diversion dam. Only an hour paddling later and we were at the end of our journey. There was no tumultuous explosion of uncontrolled emotions or hysterical congratulations. There was instead a warm good feeling inside that we had completed the trip—a trip that by our calculations covered 500 miles of river and passed through 6 counties. Best of all, no one was injured or snakebite."

James Durden on the end of the trip
"After a nights rest, early the following morning, we returned to move the second canoe. When we got back to the canoe we'd

Confluence of Guadalupe and San Antonio Rivers

left behind—we were shocked to discover that *our machetes had been stolen.* This was most unnerving inasmuch as we thought we were alone in this wilderness. To discover that there were not only unidentified people around—but those *people were now seriously armed with our machetes!*

"Rather quickly, we moved the second canoe and I remember there was a lot of head turning and watching our backside going on with an ever-growing sense of uneasiness.

"We never did recover our machetes nor did we ever see anyone during the portage. I for one was glad to be back on the water and en route down river.

"Ultimately, it was the logjams that made us decide to end our journey at the Tivoli Bridge at the entrance of San Antonio Bay. We had earlier entertained the notion of finishing the trip by entering Guadalupe Bay. We had to face the *obvious truth*: It looked like it was going to be one logjam after another the rest of the way to the bay. The repeated portaging required more energy then we had left. We were also aware that our fresh water canoes with their low bows were not suitable for bay use where large waves required the use of splash shields.

"And so, when we finally reached the bridge at Tivoli, we decided by unanimous vote that this would be the official end of our trip. It was without any sadness whatsoever. Our goal had been to challenge ourselves and have fun in the process. Part of that challenge was making good decisions when good decisions were necessary. The decision to stop at the Tivoli Bridge was a smart decision."

A final word from Peter Krauter:

"We raised our paddles in a salute to the end of our journey. I remember how silent everyone was as we pondered what we had just accomplished, and how future adventures yet to unfold in life would compare to the current one. Looking back now, some 35 years later, I would not have traded that experience for anything in the world, and I'm still thankful to all our parents for allowing and supporting us in the pursuit of our dream, and to my comrades in adventure. We will always share a special link from our experiences for the remainder of our lives."

The Spirit of the Journey: James

"As we approached the point of our landing at the Tivoli Bridge I knew I had succeeded in all my promises to myself and for me that was an extremely good feeling! As it ended up there was no race to the finish or even any desire exhibited by any one of us to be the first to cross some imaginary line. In fact, the night prior to the end of our trip we had discussed the finish and determined that it would only be fair and proper that we finish the trip together. With this spirit in mind, we pulled the two canoes together, side by side, and drifted into the landing at the bridge with paddles held upwards reminiscent of the ancient Vikings. We completed our trip in the spirit of friendship and camaraderie that comes from achieving something truly great as the result of team work."

We pulled the canoes side by side and drifted into the landing at the bridge at Tivoli with paddles held upwards reminiscent of the ancient Vikings. We completed our trip in the spirit of friendship and camaraderie that comes from achieving something truly great as the result of teamwork.—James

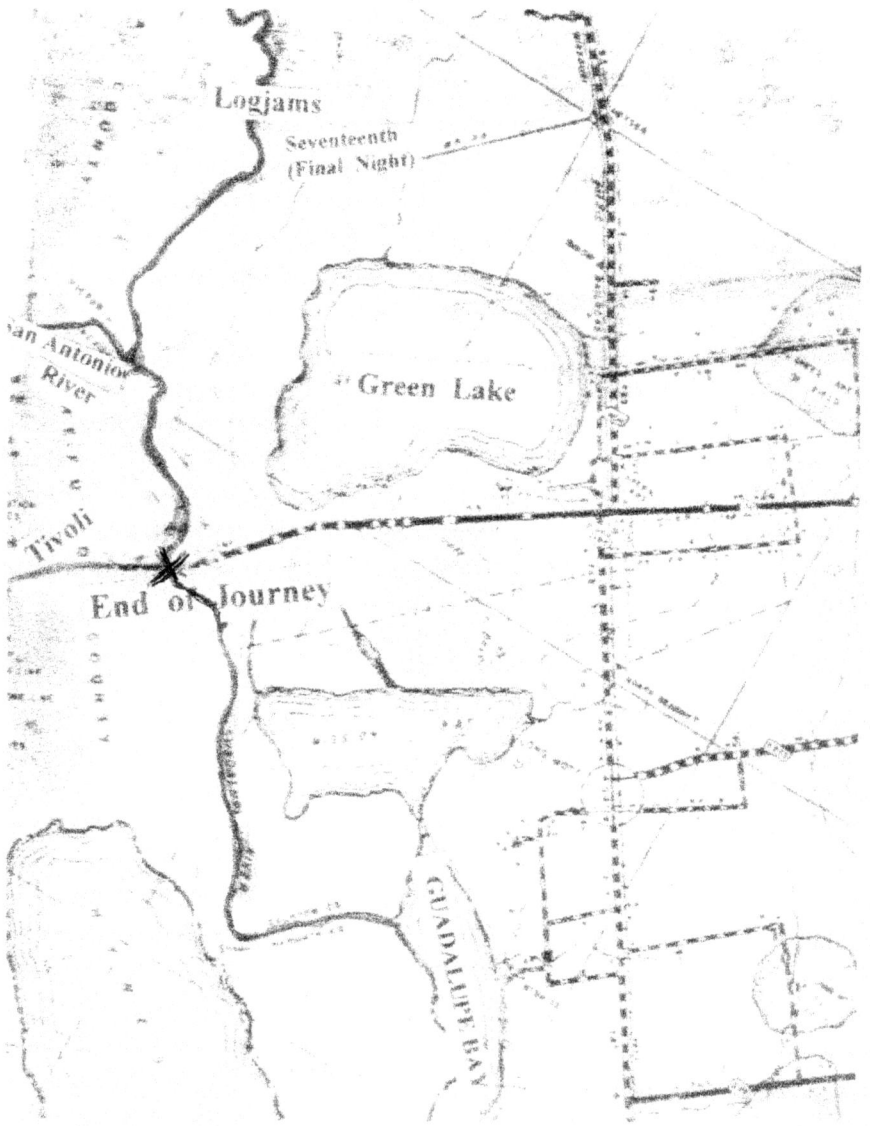

End of the journey

Matagorda Island State Park & Wildlife Management Area

End of the journey

Epilogue

Back to Don's Journal

"Peter and James decided to hitchhike into Tivoli while Mark and I waited with the canoes. They only took several steps away from our canoes and decided their *body odor* was so bad that they'd better remove their shirts ..."

James and Peter

"Once we landed at Tivoli and got a make shift sort of camp set up Peter and I climbed up to the highway to walk into Tivoli to find a telephone to call our parents and tell them the good news. It was not all that far into Tivoli from the Guadalupe River Bridge but for two guys who have just come 500 very "wet" miles to the coast—the prospect of a two mile hike was looking like a marathon. Things were beginning to—no—that's not right—things were agonizingly chaffed! So, it was almost like manna from heaven when a truck stopped and offered us a lift into town. *We hadn't even taken half a dozen steps.* See, that's how this whole trip was! When there was a desperate need— *something always seemed to appear from somewhere.* Call it the guardian angel—good karma—or the power of positive thinking—whichever you prefer. The fact is, whatever we needed, it was always there.

"When we came to the first house we asked to be dropped off and we knocked on the door. A young girl came to open it and we asked if we could use their telephone. Her mother took

136

one look at us and said, "No." We continued to walk. Finally, an old black man in an old Chevy truck gave us a ride all the way into town—it was only about a mile.

"We located a pay phone and gave our moms and dads a call letting them know we had arrived safely and were waiting for a ride home.

"Knowing that it would be several hours before the cavalry arrived, we loaded up on chips, sodas, and candy bars from the Tivoli convenience store and headed back to the river. Once again, with little to no effort on our part, a friendly fellow picked us up and dropped us off at the bridge.

"To this day I cannot remember what we did those four hours while waiting for our parents to arrive. Maybe we just slept—or repacked things for the ride home—or just sat and talked—I really don't know. I don't remember any great celebration for having accomplished something pretty bold and unusual. Nor do I remember being sad that the trip was over and that it would be life as usual once back in Comfort. I do remember having a very good feeling. I remember being happy. I think I also remembered wondering if this might give me an edge over some of the other less fortunate guys in Comfort (who didn't have a canoe trip to talk about) when it came to dating the young ladies around Comfort. Ah yes—amazing what goes on inside the mind of a 15 year old!

"After four hours our parents arrived at Tivoli and we had our joyous reunions. We quickly packed everything into the auto trunks, loaded the canoes on top, and headed for home. Our parents complained that we stunk! Imagine that ... four guys ... two canoes ... and all those glorious days in the great outdoors on the river ... and our parents thought we *stank*! I can only imagine how we must have reeked of sweat and that awful river mud that was filled with rotting and decaying matter. Yippers!

"But, Peter's Grandmother Ingenhuett was apparently pretty impressed with this achievement by her grandson and his gang. She accompanied his mom on the long drive to Tivoli and insisted on paying for a steak dinner for us all.

One would think Vera Rausch was happy to see son Mark!

We drove to Victoria before we could find a restaurant still open at this late hour. My mom went inside to see the manager first, to tell him who we were and warned him of our "physical condition" and would they consider letting us come inside to feed us. The manager was very excited and said, "You bring those boys in here. They deserve a good steak!"

Mark Rausch gathers up paddles for long auto trip back to Comfort, Texas. It was around 9:00 P.M.

Four river rats ready to go home!

"I remember the food! I had a chicken fried steak with French fries and ketchup. Warm fries with ketchup! Can there be a better combination?"

Once we were underway again and on our final leg back to Comfort, we literally passed out and slept all the way home.

Once the canoers were back in Comfort, Dave Andrews of KERV, the radio station in Kerrville, called to ask if he could come to Comfort to interview the boys. Naturally, they agreed. [*The Comfort News* was sponsored by Marie's Variety Store and The Comfort State Bank.]

The priceless recording of that interview still exists on a cassette. Priceless because it has a recording of Mark's mother and Peter's mom! (both since deceased)

What is precious about the interview is when Dave Andrews asked Don and Peter why they had wanted to make this trip, the answers came around the circle. Don said, "I've thought about

Yellowed 1971 Comfort News *carried this front page news showing the "Trailblazers" in café at Victoria.*

this trip ever since elementary school. The really serious thinking started in January of this year."

Peter Krauter replied, "At least three to four years ago I started thinking about a canoe trip down the Guadalupe. I never thought it would ever happen."

James Durden and Mark Rausch laughed and replied, "We really just wanted to get out of the house!"

When Mr Andrews asked Don why the idea was so intriguing, he replied, "I always wondered what it would be like living off the land when making a journey like this. We didn't do that and I'm sure glad we didn't have to!"

Another interesting question put to the boys was about their calculations of the miles of river they'd traveled. {Most research had shown that the river was from 200 to 250 miles long.} "We kept our daily record and it was more like 450 to 500 miles that we paddled."

Mr Andrews ended the program with a salute to the four teenage boys saying they should not be called boys any longer, but should now be called "young men."

The morning after arriving home:

Little brother Roger Durden smiles widely to have his two brothers home again. Don and James, no worse for the wear, seem ready to plan their next journey.

Little brother, Roger Durden, smiles widely because his big brothers are home again!

"Friends to the end" are Don, James, Mark and Peter.

Thirty-six Years Later:
Biographies of the Four Today

Don Durden

DON DURDEN

After returning from the June 1971 canoe trip, Don Durden returned to Comfort High School, graduating in 1972 as salutatorian of his class. He then attended Texas Lutheran College (now Texas Lutheran University) in Seguin, Texas, on a scholarship pursuing a pre-architecture curriculum.

In August of 1974, with the Guadalupe River in the background, Don and his high school sweetheart, Susan Rose, were married at Susan's home. After a brief honeymoon, they lived in a small mobile home in College Station, Texas, where they both attended Texas A&M University. They graduated in 1977, Susan with a BA degree in Educational Curriculum and Instruction, and Don with a BS in Civil Engineering.

Don immediately began his engineering career with a small consulting engineering and surveying firm in San Antonio, Texas, and by 1981, he was licensed as a professional engineer. In 1983, he founded Civil Engineering Consultants in San Antonio, with six to eight individuals on staff. The firm prospered and soon grew to 20 employees. He incorporated the firm in 1984 as Don Durden, Inc. dba Civil Engineering Consultants. The business continues to grow and today ranks among the largest engineering firms in San Antonio.

In 1987, the Bexar Chapter of the Texas Society of Professional Engineers (TSPE) selected Don as the Young Engineer of the Year. This year, 2007, the same organization selected Don as the Engineer of the Year. He has held a variety of leadership positions in the Texas Council of Engineering

145

Companies, culminating in his service as Chairman in 2005-06. He has also been active in the Bexar Chapter of TSPE, and the local Chapter of Professional Engineers in Private Practice.

In his home town of Comfort, Don has also been involved in educational issues. In the late '80s and early '90s, he was the leader of a Citizen's Advisory Committee (an ad hoc committee formed by the Comfort ISD School Board) to offer advice regarding much needed school facility improvements. Later, in 1995, he served on the Comfort ISD Board of Trustees and was elected president in 1997, the year the district approved the bond issue to build the school facilities. He continued serving until 1999, when he resigned because of moving out of the single member district he represented. He again served as a Trustee from 2004-2006.

Meanwhile, Don has also been extensively involved in the business community, serving on a variety of Greater and North San Antonio Chamber of Commerce committees dealing primarily with legislative and infrastructure issues. In 1996, Mayor Bill Thornton appointed Don to serve on the Mayor's Water Committee, where he made significant contributions to the *Framework for Progress*, a blueprint to guide the City of San Antonio's efforts to secure an adequate supply of affordable, high quality water.

Don, a member of Gaddis Memorial United Methodist Church in Comfort, sings in the choir and serves as a Lay Speaker. He is a long time member of the Administrative Council, currently serving as Vice-Chairman. He has also chaired the Long Range Planning Committee and later the Building Committee that effected a complete relocation of the church to a new site on Highway 87 North.

Don and Susan have three sons: Chisom, who died in 1986; Jesse, currently pursuing an MBA at Texas A&M; and Dakota, currently pursuing a BS in Construction Science also at Texas A&M. Today, Don and Susan live outside of Comfort, at the same place where they were married in 1974, at the confluence of Block Creek and the Guadalupe River, where they raise hay and sheep, and two really fat cows. In addition to managing and leading CEC and farming, Don enjoys hunting, building things, reading, an occasional game of golf, and making sausage with his brothers James and Roger, their sons, and nephews. Don still enjoys canoeing from time to time, but is presently "canoe less." He loaned his canoe to a friend who unfortunately wrapped it around a tree!

THIS PERSPECTIVE FROM DON DURDEN
Thirty five years downstream.

I write this on the eve of my 53rd birthday, a few months more than thirty-five years *after* our canoe trip down the Guadalupe. In retrospect, there is *still* some residual sense of pride in knowing that we did something few others have done even though mitigated substantially that our feat pales in comparison to many others' feats.

In the overall scheme of things, this trip was but one miniscule accomplishment by four relatively obscure teenagers. Yet for those four teenage boys, it was both important and worthwhile, and for the three of us who remain, it continues to be. Why is this? I would have to say it gave me some insight into myself, about what makes me tick, about my leadership style, and the mental models I use to make sense out of life.

For example, it was an endeavor characterized by some, but not a lot of planning and preparation and a "we'll cross that bridge (or that lake, or that dam, or that whatever) when we get to it" approach to many uncertainties. I recognize this dynamic in many of my undertakings today, and I have come to understand that spontaneity offers both advantages and disadvantages.

In addition, I have observed that I hold firmly to the belief that persistence and hard work are usually as important as innate skill. Still, one cannot squeeze unscathed through episodes like *that last snake encounter* without the understanding that, in at least some cases, luck (some would say God's grace), thankfully, trumps everything else.

Third, during our trip, confronted with many situations and impediments, we had to decide how we were going to deal with them. In most cases, we did this collaboratively, drawing ideas from the entire team, evaluating them, selecting one, and then moving forward, making adjustments, if necessary, as we progressed. Concisely, this is how I approach life. I am a collaborative leader who prefers making decisions by consensus. Sometimes this takes longer than many would like, but on balance, I find complicated issues are ultimately resolved more expeditiously by *consensus decision-making processes* than they are by repeated attempts to sell or enforce autocratic decisions. Still, there are times where command and pure majority rule decisions are appropriate. In general, I believe there are always options, though in some cases, experience has shown that none of the options is good or easy.

Finally, the most important lesson I learned about myself was that I long more for the journey than for the destination. What a gift to have the presence of mind to experience gratitude for *all* of life's experiences, good, bad, and irrelevant! During the canoe trip, I was so focused on finishing the trip that I failed, I think, to appreciate each and every hour of each and every day. Still, the relentless pursuit of "the goal" is not all bad, in that the achievement of one goal allows and foments the pursuit of the next. I have yet to resolve if one can be present to the here and now and also give justice to planning for the future. This dichotomy is one of several ambiguities that make life rich for me.

One of the courses I was required to pass to earn my civil engineering degree dealt with the mathematical theories related to differential equations. This was a difficult course. We were to learn, among other things, how to *model interdependent relationships over time*. One example of such a relationship is created by placing a cup of hot coffee in a cool room: the ambient temperature of the room cools the coffee, while the hot coffee also raises the ambient temperature of the room, be it ever so slightly, until the temperature of the coffee and the room are identical. The canoe trip was that hot cup of coffee in the cool room of my life: the manner in which I approached and participated in the trip was influenced by who I was, while the trip influenced who I *am*.

Today, looking back, the most profound thing about the trip was not the accomplishment. Instead, the satisfaction comes *from responding genuinely to your heart's virtuous call.*

It is important for people to be *virtuously genuine*: to be honest about whom they are, who they are called to be, about what they believe in, and about what they will stand for and what they will stand against. My hope for my sons, and all of today's young people, is that they have the courage to be virtuously genuine. I would hope that they *follow* their heart's virtuous call. I would rejoice when they journey down life's rivers with respect for others, both those they meet along the way and those who follow them. I pray that they be sensitive to their environment, and find joy in both learning from and adapting to it, until they encounter that great confluence through which we all must pass.

MARK HUBERT RAUSCH
By Mark's sisters,
Diana Drenner and Sharon Sattler

Mark, son of Hubert and Vera Rausch, was born July 12, 1954, in Fredericksburg, Texas, and was what we Germans call *"Ein Nest Eier."* Sister Diana was twelve years older, and Sharon, four years older than Mark.

The Rausch family moved to live in the Oakcrest development in Comfort, Texas. Mark attended Comfort High School and after the canoe trip he too returned to high school where he was now a senior and the popular drummer with the high school band. He was elected treasurer of that organization and was later also crowned Mr FFA. He graduated from Comfort High School in 1972. After graduation he went to work for the Missouri Pacific-Union Pacific Railroad.

Of interest regarding his job on the railroad, essentially, Mark was a "walk in" and was hired without prior education or experience. His uncle also with the railroad, had seniority, recommended him and he secured the job. He must have pleased the boss! He was a brakeman and conductor for 17 years. He retired from the railroad in 1989, and built a home on his parent's small ranch a few miles out of Comfort.

In 1982, Mark married the former Barbara Waage of Haugesund, Norway. Mark met Barbara while she was in the United States on a work visa and working at the Fair Oaks Country Club Pro Shop—located between Boerne and San Antonio, Texas. They divorced in 1990. Mark and Barbara had

Mark Hubert Rausch

two daughters, Bjorg and Katrine, who are now grown and live in Norway.

Mark loved to hunt and fish, was an excellent swimmer, and had a personality that knew no stranger. He was very tall (6'4"). Because of this "persona," and while vacationing in Europe, he was sometimes mistaken for a celebrity (most likely Mick Jagger) and was given special treatment in restaurants and clubs.

Mark lived in Round Rock, Texas, for several years and often went swimming and boating. He and some of his friends also regularly participated in the Austin Town Lake annual canoe races. Once, while at Lake Austin, along with his German Sheppard, a man swimming alone called for help, and Mark and his dog saved this man from drowning by the man holding on to the dog's collar and Mark supporting and pushing the man from behind.

In 1994, Mark died of cancer at the young age of 40. Although his life was relatively short, he lived it to the fullest.

JAMES SHEPPARD DURDEN
Born 9/12/55

After the canoe trip that summer of 1971, fifteen-year-old James returned to Comfort High School where he continued to play football under coach Earl McKeithan. He had previously played both offense and defense on the varsity team beginning as a freshman. The team was the first Comfort football squad to win district championship in the history of Comfort High School. James continued football for the remaining three years of his high school career. He lettered every year, was named All District in his junior and senior years and received All American team honors in his senior year. James also played tennis and was good enough to go on to win district honors representing Comfort High School in UIL competition for doubles both his sophomore and junior years.

James' hobby even as a youngster was to disassemble anything electronic—*just to see what made it tick.* He was particularly fond of disassembling car radios provided to him by his great-uncle Charlie and televisions picked up from the local repair shop in Comfort. He kept his closet filled with cardboard boxes of parts extracted from these old "junkers" and spent hours tinkering with all the bits and pieces. It was only natural that that interest should draw him into the Comfort-based Southwestern Engineering Company, a telecommunications firm. And so, after graduating from Comfort High School in 1974, James immediately went to work for Southwestern Engineering Company and later Milford Engineering, both

153

James Sheppard Durden

telecommunications engineering firms providing services to independent telephone cooperatives and companies throughout the states of Texas, Oklahoma, Arkansas, Louisiana, and New Mexico. Later, and for several more years, his work in fiber optics required that he travel extensively all over the U.S. from coast to coast, from California to New York, to U.S. coastal regions and Midwest refineries and Mexico.

During this time, whenever he was available and on weekends, James served his community as a volunteer firefighter with the Comfort Volunteer Fire Department. He installed and maintained their two-way radio system and worked with them for 15 years. Meanwhile, he also studied to become an Emergency Medical Technician, but his continuing travels prevented the completion of that course.

As stated earlier, James' hobby even as a youngster was to disassemble anything electronic—*to see what made it tick*. This natural curiosity towards technology led to many unusual opportunities for James. One memorable innovation was to "fix" an old 16mm movie projector so that it could pull a miniature replica of Santa's sled across the ceiling of the elementary library where his librarian mother produced puppet shows every Christmas. Students from every grade level sat in rapt attention knowing that at some point in the puppet production the lights would go off and Santa's sled would "fly" for the Comfort Elementary Library Children's Theatre project.

Another awesome Children's Theatre "*James creation*" was built for a stage play his mother wrote and produced with fifth grade student as actors. It was during the Star Wars era and the play was a unique outer space drama that needed a R2D2 robot replica. James used blinking colored Christmas lights and a wheeled three-foot tall drum with a dome on top, complete with beeping sounds. It entered the stage being pulled by a nylon rope. It was another "*show stopper*"!

It was not long before computers presented James with a new challenge. He studied the technology until there was no mystery left for him. He soon astounded those around him with his working knowledge of what made them tick. He became a patient teacher and understanding technician when it came to "fixing" things that those of lesser understanding had messed up.

It was no surprise then when eventually James brought his expertise in technology back home. Thus, in 1998, after 24 years spent in the air and on the road, James joined his brother Don's firm, Civil Engineering Consultants of San Antonio, Texas, and the Durden brothers were back together again. Today James is the Information Technology Manager of Civil Engineering Consultants in San Antonio, Texas, where Don is the CEO.

Today James, the father of a son, Joshua, and a daughter, Kristin, still lives in Comfort, Texas, where they as a family continue to enjoy all the gifts that the old Guadalupe River has to offer. Like their dad, Josh and Kristin are both avid anglers and love to spend Saturday evenings on the river swimming or just camping out and enjoying the outdoors together.

James is also part owner of the Durden family ranch in Gillespie County. Sometime during the '70s, he and his dad, Jerry Durden, built an awesome and very creative fireplace of rustic rock they found on the ranch, to compliment the weekend cabin which the entire family built as a weekend project. It took five years of dissembling old structures and reassembling new ones from the recovered materials before the beautiful cabin was finally completed in 1978. Today the ranch house sits proudly atop a small knoll and offers a grand view into Gillespie, Mason, Kimble, and other Texas counties of the Llano Estacada.

James has also done vast research into ranch conservation practices and wildlife management. He has spent many weekend hours on the ranch tractor breaking up formerly uncultivated land and preparing food plots for white-tailed deer. He enjoys hunting, fishing, and every winter making sausages with his brothers, Don and Roger, his kids, Josh and Kristin, and nephews, Dakota and Jesse.

LOOKING BACK ON THE
CANOE JOURNEY EXPERIENCE
By James Sheppard Durden

One of the most definitive things that comes to mind about the trip was that it was a lot of paddling! I really do not know or cannot remember why it seemed like we were *always in such a big hurry* but paddle stroke was followed by paddle stroke and it seemed we had very little time for anything else. Please don't misunderstand, it's not like there wasn't time to look around and take in the sights. Canoe travel, at least on the Guadalupe River, is slow business. The old Guadalupe snakes around the coastal plain of Texas like it would rather *not* reach the Gulf, preferring to stay in the scenic area known as the Texas Hill Country. The river seems to get lazy and slow and I'd swear, if the wind was blowing up-river you'd come to a dead stop if you stopped paddling.

Overall for me, and I think for the other guys as well, the part that kept us moving was that there was always the anticipation of discovering what was just around the bend. Perhaps this is something similar to what motivated the early pioneers to press on to the Pacific Ocean; the allure of getting even a peek at what lay just ahead was stronger then their sense of misery. They endured freezing blizzards, dry dusty deserts, and endless miles of prairie boredom. That same sense drove us just as it drove the early explorers.

Sure, we had *maps*! But maps can only tell part of the story. On our two-dimensional maps, what we *discovered* did not match what we *imagined*. Things like horseshoe-bends in the river. We thought miles of river could be avoided by simply portaging that small strip of land we saw on the map separating the tips of the horseshoe. We had a good plan in theory and on paper. But an impossible plan when we discovered that small strip of land separating the tips was terrain actually two or three hundred feet straight up and straight back down making portage completely out of the question! It was humbling to say the least and it presented a challenge for patience. This alone ended up being a source of conquest and pride to put it in its proper perspective. We grumbled a little at first at being fooled by Mother Nature, but we paddled around that horseshoe just like that had been the original plan all along. Nothing seemed insurmountable and every problem solved added fuel to our determination.

We all grew a bit more mature during our trip down the river. We learned to adapt and to do whatever was necessary whether anticipated or not. We learned to make the most out of whatever we found and we learned to do it with a *good sense of humor*. Thirty-five years later, it is the laughter and the fun that I recall, not the hardships and the burdens.

On wanting to go again...

Of all the Texas Rivers I've experienced, none can compare to the Guadalupe. Granted, the Guadalupe is by far the most familiar to me, and the one I have seen the most often. But, in my opinion this river has an *individual character* that can never be duplicated by any other. True, the Medina, Sabinal, Rio Frio, and many other Texas rivers all have cypress trees along their length but none of them can compare to the beauty and majesty of the cypress trees that line the Guadalupe. In addition, yes, the Pedernales and the Llano and the Colorado and many other Texas rivers all have ancient pecan trees growing in the fertile soils that have washed out of the hills located in their watersheds. But the pecans that line the Guadalupe—mixed as they are with cypress and the cottonwoods and the willows and the countless other plant species—all combine along the banks of the Guadalupe River to create an environment as peaceful and serene as any that have ever existed. The relatively low flow rate of the Guadalupe—with its tumultuous limestone transversal—has created a river that is both exciting and challenging to navigate with a mood that is slow moving and soothing to the soul. From gravel bars to sandy banks to hard limestone ledges, the river twists and turns as the result of eons and eons of continuingly finding the path of least resistance. You will see narrow channels cut deep into solid rock and huge boulders tossed about randomly during repeated flooding episodes. These random boulders, worn limestone ridges, gravel bars and abundant trees all work together to create a canoeist's paradise. One moment you are being swept along by the river's current as it twists and turns and falls head-long over and around ancient limestone formations and the next you are having to pull mightily on your paddle just to keep the canoe going in the right direction even as the current seems to ebb and want to go back up-river.

And, basically the Guadalupe is a clean river too. Sure we saw some pollution; I doubt if there's any river that hasn't been exposed to development and not been used as a conduit for the removal of human and animal waste. But, the Guadalupe River has a mechanism to prevent the accumulation of waste which would otherwise render it unusable. It's called *flooding* and it works very, very well. Typically, significant rains that occur in the upper expanses of the Texas Hill Country swiftly runs off the steep limestone hills of this part of Texas. This runoff collects in draws and gullies, flowing into canyons, valleys and creeks until it all comes together in the Guadalupe River to begin its journey to the sea. These "high water" events which typically occur in the spring and fall seasons effectively cleans the river of its deposited waste sediments and leaves behind the washed gravel bars, smoothly worn limestone ridges, and cleanly defined banks that make up the river today.

There are also natural springs, recharged by the heavy rains that supply the river with crystal clean, cold, fresh water. Springs sustain the river between the rainy seasons and this effect yields a river of awesome beauty especially in the area above Canyon Lake. There are high towering, smoothly worn rock walls along the outside bank of the bends in the river while the inside has magnificent cypress or pecan trees that must have been growing there since the beginning of time. As the river cuts deeper and deeper into the soft limestone rock that forms its bottom it finds voids, fissures, and cracks of which it takes advantage. Sometimes the spring spills straight ahead through a narrow slot that once may have been no more then a mere crack in the rock but today is a deeply cut channel.

Progressing around the next bend, the river might take an abrupt left or a right as the flow runs headlong into impervious stone only to find an exit through or around a soft spot elsewhere ... the awesome horseshoe bends!

As you progress farther and farther down the river the effects of the flood cleanings become harder and harder to find. Probable cause may be man's efforts to tame the river and manage its flood-time flow to reduce property damage. There the river has become somewhat polluted. Sadly, now the river's path also becomes a bit less wild as well, making wide, slow curving turns instead of jumping from this direction to that. Overall though, it's still a beautiful, graceful old river. She just needs a chance to breathe and run occasionally to keep things moving along.

I've thought many times, *man, I wish we could do that 1971 canoe trip again*! But, in retrospect, I doubt that it would ever, or could ever, be the same. The sensation of not knowing what was next or how we would handle this predicament or that obstacle could not possibly be the same the second time. Much of the pride I felt after this trip was not so much that we had *done it* but that we had managed to conduct ourselves in a way that demonstrated that *we could do it*. Sure, we did some dumb things on our trip. We were kids and pretty darn near immortal. Nevertheless, we also did some really intelligent and sensible things as well. And as teenagers growing up in the early 1970s and with the possibility of military duty in Vietnam looming on each of our horizons, I think it was of the utmost importance that we each *demonstrated to ourselves* that we had what was necessary to survive whatever. This trip presented each of us with our own very personal set of challenges and each of us successfully overcame them.

Would I recommend this trip to other young men and women today? Absolutely! The challenges may be different but the objective is the same ... set yourself a goal and achieve it.

Whether it's just to go for a day or two or for the full length, it will be time extremely well spent and give you stories to talk about for the rest of your lives.

Several important things to consider if you plan to canoe the Guadalupe River:

1) I recommend the canoes we used made by Grumman especially for the Boy Scouts. They are cargo canoes with relatively wide flat bottoms and adequate bracing to carry a large amount of gear amidship. They give good performance and are a definite asset in a traversal such as Canyon Lake. Their draft is minimal, their keel is strong, and their stability extraordinary.

2) The canoes have solid aluminum seats which provided more then adequate support and durability. But, be forewarned, they can get hard by the end of the day ... especially when the water is deep and slow and the portaging infrequent. Seriously consider taking along some extra burlap sacks to use as seat cushions. Your rump will thank you!

3) Thankfully, Peter had the presence of mind to take a camera along on our trip. All the pictures in this book came from his camera. We still regret not having more visuals of what we saw and what we encountered. Take lots of cameras, batteries, and memory sticks; you're going to need them!

4) Approach the river with respect. While she can be as tranquil and graceful as a ballerina, she can also be as deadly as two trains colliding at full steam. Our experience on the river was successful but not all who have gone down to the river in boats were so lucky. Many have paid the ultimate price because they were not aware and cognizant of the fact that the river is and can be a very dangerous place.

Conclusion:

I can never say enough about the kindness and support of

our parents, Bob Roberts, and all the people we ran into on the river. Everyone we met was a testimony to the true spirit of what it means to be a Texan. They were friendly, helpful, and genuinely concerned that we should succeed. To all of them I say, Thank you!

And to Don, Mark, and Peter: You all know that I've never been much for mushy sentimentality but for the record I'd like it to conclude here that I sincerely thank each one of you for allowing me the opportunity to have participated in this adventure. Your individual personalities on this trip enriched the experience for me and made the way so much easier. *Don*, your ability to organize and manage people was starting to show even then. You kept us all marching in line and motivated. *Peter*, your keen sense of nature and feel for the land added immensely to the trip. And *Mark*, your sense of humor and antics kept us laughing and in high spirits even when we should have dropped in our tracks. Who can *ever* forget the motto you coined for us: *"Still tastes like damn river water!"* Mark so loved to say it!

While today we've each gone our separate ways, those seventeen days spent with you all will, without a doubt, be the most memorable experience of my life. God bless you all and keep you all forever sheltered under the wings of His angels.

PETER C. KRAUTER

My love of travel and adventure did not end with the canoe trip down the Guadalupe. I was blessed with the opportunity to participate in a five-week educational study tour of eight European countries while still in high school along with a number of my classmates. After graduating from Comfort High School in 1974, I received an Associate in Arts degree from Schreiner College ('76) and received a full scholarship in engineering to Southern Methodist University from Texas Instrumentsâ.

I soon realized the '70s-era culture of Biff, Buffy, polo shirts, and Datsun 240Z's was not where I wanted to be, and engineering was not as interesting to me as the biotic world. I enrolled at Texas A&M University in January 1977, earning Bachelor and Master of Science degrees in Entomology from Texas A&M University in '79 and '87, respectively. Upon entering graduate school in 1979, I accepted the position of Research Associate in the "Biological Control and IPM of Cotton Insect Pests" project at Texas A&M University, wherein I participated for fifteen years in foreign exploration for natural enemies of insect pests in the forests and mountains of Mexico south to Panama. Now approaching 28 years of service at Texas A&M University, I am involved in research and extension activities related to greenhouse and ornamental pest management as a specialist in biological control and integrated pest management.

I currently reside in Bryan, Texas, with my wife, Marianna,

Peter C. Krauter

and two daughters, Johanna (11) and Jamie (8), with whom I spend most of my free time experiencing the discovery of life all over again through their eyes.

My Perspective of the Canoe Trip After 35 Years
Peter C. Krauter

I cannot help but wonder how different a trip down the Guadalupe would be today. Just as James made reference to the movie *Deliverance*, many others who have heard our tale have alluded to the fears inspired by that film which was released the year following our trip. In retrospect, a comparison of the two tales reveals two opposite experiences. Burt Reynolds and cast embarked upon their adventure to experience the river wild and untamed before construction of a new hydroelectric dam was completed, but were entrapped in some rather unsavory human interactions. Our trip was not undertaken with the expectation that the river would soon be physically altered, but rather as an endeavor of human spirit and love for nature. Our interactions with the people we met along the way were positive and enriching.

While the physical character of the Guadalupe River has not changed much over the past 35 years, the people along its banks have been altered dramatically by ever increasing numbers, selfishness, and fear of litigation. Although the riverbed belongs to the citizens of Texas, access to the river and, therefore, the enjoyment of the river, is increasingly being restricted as the population of Texas grows out of control and increasingly expensive land along the river passes to new owners. Locations on the upper Guadalupe where multiple generations enjoyed the cool, refreshing waters of the Guadalupe River on a scorching, Sunday afternoon in the summer are no longer conveniently accessible, if at all, to the public.

Our trip was mostly one of solitude, encountering very few people or associated garbage during the long stretches of river between communities. We even joked once that we must be getting close to a town when we saw one aluminum can and some spent shotgun shells floating near some brush along the bank of the river, which turned out to be a correct assumption. This most surely has changed with the many subdivisions and residential developments having been built along the river basin.

With the exception of the first nights' encounter with a relatively recent landowner who made it clear we were not welcome to spend the night along "their" stretch of river, or the scoundrels who took it upon themselves to relieve us of our machetes when we left them unattended, every person we encountered was warm, friendly, and helpful, representing the best stereotypical qualities attributed to Texans. Some were generous beyond expectation, such as the McCurdys who generously gave us shelter in a storm, the owner who let us spend the night in his old power plant, and even the fisherman who gave us a short tow in the headwaters of Canyon Lake when the light of day was fading. I would like to believe those people still exist along the rivers of Texas, but have become increasingly skeptical over the years.

Why did we set out to take the journey down the Guadalupe River? As I recall, we never set out to simulate the hardships of the early explorers of Texas, but rather to experience a journey to explore our own physical and mental limits of endurance and desire for adventure. What we ended up with was a priceless experience in teamwork, camaraderie, and self-reliance. I would wish this type of experience upon every young person who has the required courage and fortitude, as well as understanding and supporting parents.

THE END

About the Author

Alora (Mae) Durden-Nelson retired in 1997 after twenty-seven years as the Comfort School District's elementary children's librarian where she also authored and produced puppet, marionette, and/or stage plays twice a year, every year, with fifth and sixth grade students for her Elementary Library Children's Theater project. One play, *The Case of the Easter Villians*, was published by *Plays Inc.* magazine. Meanwhile, she also served on several community service boards including the Comfort Public Library, elected president in 1995, and served until her retirement from public school. She is presently on the Comfort Public Education Foundation board, writes public relations news articles, and serves on their scholarship committee. The Rising Star Masonic Lodge of Center Point, Texas has honored her with a Community Builder Award. Durden-Nelson is a member of the Southwest Chapter of Book Writers and Illustrators.

Her earlier writing credits include being a stringer/freelance reporter and Society Editor for the *Kerrville Daily Times*; she compiled and wrote the history of the Immanuel Lutheran Church in Comfort, *With Eternal Glory* and authored two newspaper series for the *Comfort News* on the "History of the Comfort PTA" and "Why Voter Registration?"

Durden-Nelson's first retirement-writing project, requested by the YMCA in 1999, was to research the history of the 1,100 acre Robert's Ranch near Comfort and then produce a brochure for the ranch as a Boy and Girl Scout primitive camping site and to encourage field trips for educational, historical, archeological, rock-climbing and birding adventures.

Durden-Nelson's first book, *I Just Called Her Momma*, contracted by Eakin Press in 2000, was published in 2003 and she has written and published a book a year ever since: *Son of Defiance* (2004), *Genesis–Beginning Again* (2005), and *When Saints Go Marching*, (2006). *Four Boys, Two Canoes, and the Guadalupe River* (2007) is her fifth book.

For more information on this author see www.maedurden nelson.com

www.ingramcontent.com/pod-product-compliance
Lightning Source LLC
Chambersburg PA
CBHW070837100426
42813CB00003B/657